Anti-inflammatory Diet Cookbook for Beginners

Reduce the Inflammation and Improve your Health with over 1000 Days of Quick & Easy Recipes | 60-Days Smart Meal Plan Included!

Lora M. Stoops

© Copyright 2022 by Lora M. Stoops - All rights reserved.

This document is geared towards providing exact and reliable information in regard to the topic and issue covered.

- From a Declaration of Principles which was accepted and approved equally by a Committee of the American Bar Association and a Committee of Publishers and Associations.

In no way is it legal to reproduce, duplicate, or transmit any part of this document in either electronic means or in printed format. All rights reserved.

The information provided herein is stated to be truthful and consistent, in that any liability, in terms of inattention or otherwise, by any usage or abuse of any policies, processes, or directions contained within is the solitary and utter responsibility of the recipient reader. Under no circumstances will any legal responsibility or blame be held against the publisher for any reparation, damages, or monetary loss due to the information herein, either directly or indirectly.

Respective authors own all copyrights not held by the publisher.

The information herein is offered for informational purposes solely and is universal as so. The presentation of the information is without contract or any type of guarantee assurance.

The trademarks that are used are without any consent, and the publication of the trademark is without permission or backing by the trademark owner. All trademarks and brands within this book are for clarifying purposes only and are owned by the owners themselves, not affiliated with this document.

Table of Contents

INTRODUCTION 7
LIST OF ANTI-INFLAMMATORY FOODS 11
Breakfast 12
- Muffin With Spinach And Cayenne Pepper . 12
- Morning Hazelnut Piadine 12
- Pudding With Blackcurrant And Mint 13
- Banana Pancakes With Apricots 13
- Quinoa Bread With Pecan Walnut Butter 14
- Oat Flakes With Pears And Blueberries 14
- Millet Cake With Plums 15
- Soy Cream With Asparagus 15
- Pumpkin Sweet 16
- Dried Fruit Breakfast Bars 16
- Pudding Of Apricots And Hazelnuts 17
- Baskets Of Lentils And Carrots 17
- Brown Rice Cream 18
- Crepes Of Chickpeas And Spinach 18
- Frittata With Zucchini 19

Salads 20
- Eggplant And Pomegranate Salad 20
- Salad Of Fennel, Pecan Walnuts And Blueberries 20
- Rocket And Asparagus Salad 21
- Artichokes And Pears Salad 21
- Fresh Summer Salad 22
- Autumn Salad 22
- Salad With Red Cabbage 23
- Exotic Salad 23
- Fennel And Celery Salad 24
- Salad of Cucumbers and Soy Yogurt 24
- Greek Salad 25
- Mixed Salad With Quinoa Bread 25
- Salad Of Celeriac 26
- Radish And Hazelnut Salad 26
- Aromatic Salad 27
- Salad Of Pastinaca And Red Beans 27
- Goji Berry Salad 28
- Spicy Salad 28
- Cucumber And Pomegranate Salad 29
- Green Beans And Pine Nuts Salad 29

Soups 30
- Orange Soup 30
- Spicy Pumpkin Soup 30
- Soup Of Black Beans And Zucchini 31
- Lentils And Turmeric Soup 31
- Buckwheat Soup And Onions 32
- Cauliflower And Tempeh Soup 32
- Broccoli And Brown Pear Soup 33
- Saffron Artichokes Soup 33
- Chestnut And Bean Soup 34
- Turnip And Spelled Soup 34
- Topinambur And Potato Soup 35
- Spinach And Kale Soup 35
- Spinach And Broccoli Soup 36
- Bean Soup And Lemon 36
- Pearl Barley And Red Beans Soup 37
- Soup Of Mushrooms And Tempeh 37
- Cauliflower And Miso Soup 38
- Asparagus And Tamari Soup 38
- Spinach And Corn Flour Soup 39
- Pomegranate And Pistachio Soup 39

Pasta & Cereals 40
- Buckwheat With Broccoli, Zucchini And Aubergines 40
- Basmati Rice With Peppers 40
- Quinoa With Figs And Peppers 41
- Wholemeal Pasta With Tofu, Pine Nuts And Leek 41
- Wholemeal Spaghetti With Cod And Parsley And Garlic Sauce 42
- Barley Tomatoes, Capers And Anchovies 42
- Wholemeal Pasta With Avocado And Apple 43
- Barley, Olives And Tofu 43
- Buckwheat Gnocchi With Salmon And Shrimps 44
- Millet With Tuna And Broccoli 44
- Rice With Aubergines And Octopus 45

Wholemeal Pasta And Shiitake Mushrooms. 45
Baked Wholemeal Pasta Gratin 46
Kamut With Green Beans And Saffron Mushrooms 46
Rice With Chicken And Broccoli.................... 47
Bulgur With Edamame Beans And Sprouts... 47
Venus Rice With Mackerel And Tomatoes ... 48
Wholemeal Spaghetti With Pears, Cashews And Asparagus 48
Pasta With Anchovies, Broccoli And Pecan Nuts 49
Quinoa With Totani Dried Tomatoes And Chickpeas 49
Farro With Zucchini, Tuna And Leek 50
Wholemeal Rice With Pumpkin, Ghee And Nuts 50
Wholemeal Pasta With Walnut Pesto, Pecan Basil And Dried Tomatoes............................. 51
Wholemeal Pasta With Zucchini Flowers, Tomatoes, Anchovies And Pine Nuts 51
Spicy Quinoa Cauliflower And Almonds 52

Vegetarians... 53

Salt Cake With Asparagus And Mushroom Cream... 53
Sweet Potatoes In Sweet And Sour Sauce... 53
Quenelle Of Cannellini Beans With Hummus And Parsley Cream 54
Rice Paper Rolls With Broccoli And Tofu 54
Zucchini Fritters With Garlic Sauce 55
White Onions Filled With Rice 55
Sweet Potato Carpaccio With Cremini Mushroom Cream 56
Tempeh With Ginger Sauce 56
Spinach With Leek And Hazelnuts.................. 57
Algae Chips.. 57
Artichokes And Beet Frittata 58
Greek Feta With Tomatoes And Almond Pesto 58
Potato Croquettes With Pumpkin Seeds....... 59
Artichokes Flan... 59
Rolls Of Quinoa Lettuce And Raspberries 60
Tempeh With Olives And Capers................... 60
Pastinache With Broccoli Cream.................... 61
Chutney Of Red Onions, Turnip And Apples 61
Piadine With Tofu And Berries....................... 62
Hamburger Of Black Rice & Chickpeas 62

Vegan... 63

Curry Pastinache Cream With Leek And Black Beans 63
Pasta With Chestnut Ragout 63
Pumpkin With Miso And Nuts........................ 64
Nugget Of Zucchini... 64
Zucchini Filled With Hummus And Spinach .. 65
Millet Meatballs With Broccoli 65
Farro With Grilled Vegetables 66
Couscous With Mixed Vegetables 66
Buckwheat With Pistachios And Raisins 67
Pistachio And Pecan Walnuts Granola For Breakfast.. 67
Seitan Stew With Olives.................................. 68
Avocado Stuffed With Spicy Chickpeas And Tofu... 68
Piadine Of Chickpeas With Spinach And Mayonnaise 69
Crunchy Balls Of Garlic Potatoes 69
Caramelized Turnip With Hazelnuts 70
Cream Of Lentils And Sweet Potatoes 70
Green Beans With Coconut And Almonds .. 71
Banana Muffin 71
Turmeric Sandwiches 72
Spelled Pasta With Grapes And Lemon 72

Fish & Seafood 73

Salmon With Rocket Pesto............................ 73
Wholemeal Rice With Cod And Pine Nuts.... 73
Cabbage With Anchovies 74
Tuna Croutons.. 74
Wholemeal Pasta With Sardines And Leeks . 75
Salmon Salad With Mushrooms And Broccoli 75
Hake With Caper Sauce And Dried Tomatoes 76
Sole Fillets With Fennel In Paperboard 76
Brown Rice With Tuna, Peppers And Rocket 77
Cod And Pumpkin Fishballs With White Sauce 77
Quinoa With Tuna Pesto 78
Mackerel With Sesame And Soy Sprouts 78
Soup Of Oysters And Mushrooms 79

Millet With Asparagus, Almonds And Sardines 79
Rolls Of Aubergines With Cod With Mediterranean Aromas 80
Tomatoes Stuffed With Tuna And Chickpeas 80
Seaweed Fritters Nori And Carrots 81
Cod With Creamy Onions 81
Cod In Grapefruit Cups 82
Squid Rings With Saffron 82
Clams With Chickpeas.....................................83
Sauce For Croutons With Salmon 83

Snacks 84
Quinoa And Lemon Cookies............................84
Sticks With Sesame And Turmeric 84
Celery With Curry Sauce 85
Apple And Cinnamon Chips............................85
Skewers Of Tofu And Zucchini........................86
Rösti Potatoes With Rosemary........................86
Chestnut Panini With Fennels 87
Sweets With Carrots And Chocolate 87
Oat Bars With Cocoa And Honey 88
Sesame And Paprika Crackers 88
Pear And Cinnamon Pudding 89
Turmeric Focaccia With Nuts 89
Peanut Butter Toast With Vegetables 90
Strawberries, Lemon And Mint 90
Oranges Stuffed With Banana And Blueberries 91
Banana And Hazelnut Cookies......................91

Smoothies & Juices 92
Acai Smoothie 92
Spirulina Smoothie And Fresh Fruit 92
Watermelon & Lemongrass Smoothie 93
Morning Smoothie 93
Mango & Dragon Fruit Smoothie...................94
Smoothie Papaya & Pineapple 94
Almond & Carrots Smoothie 95
Green Smoothie 95
Almond & Orange Smoothie 96
Beet And Mango Smoothie 96

Strawberries Hazelnuts Smoothie 97
Beet And Apple Smoothie 97
Peaches And Kiwi Smoothie 98
Smoothie With Green Cabbage And Apple 98
Smoothie Tofu And Strawberries 99
Smoothie With Oats And Apricots 99
Smoothie Mandarins And Grapefruit 100
Smoothie With Lychees And Banana 100
Red Currant Juice 101
Smoothie With Black Currants 101
Juice With Pomegranate And Raspberries 102
Juice With Winter Melon And Blueberries... 102

Dessert 103
Yellow Cake 103
Chocolate And Cherries Cake.....................103
Date And Apricot Cake 104
Almond And Hazelnut Cake 104
Beet Brownie 105
Wholemeal Rice Pudding With Plums 105
Cake With Wild Berries 106
Pecan Walnut Pralines 106
Chocolate Cream With Kiwi And Hazelnuts 107
Cookies With Peanut Butter And Sesame Seeds 107
Ice Cream Cake With Raspberries 108
Baked Apples With Crumble 108
Apricot Cake 109
Pumpkin And Dates Cake............................109
Sorbet With Honey And Goji Berries 110
Mint Chocolates 110
Peach Muffin..111
Ice Lollies With Cherry And Kiwi 111
Chestnut And Chocolate Cookies...............112
Pears Cake 112

61 Days Meal Plan..113
FAQ 119
Conversion Table...120
REFERENCES..122

INTRODUCTION

WHAT IS THE ANTI-INFLAMMATORY DIET?

The anti-inflammatory diet is a way of life. This type of meal plan involves the daily consumption of foods rich in antioxidants, omega-3 fatty acids and fiber. Many studies confirm that the anti-inflammatory diet is a real ally for our health. If it is followed consistently over time it is able to reduce or eliminate the inflammations that favor chronic diseases such as arthritis, gastritis, Crohn's disease, ulcerative colitis in the most severe cases and premature aging, general malaise, cardiovascular aging and much more in the lightest cases.

BENEFITS OF THE ANTI-INFLAMMATORY DIET

The anti-inflammatory diet can help you improve many symptoms.

Continuous use of foods that contain omega-3 fatty acids, ginger, turmeric, green tea, fruit and vegetables, nuts and seeds can lower the level of body inflammation. It is very important to learn to choose what we decide to eat every single day, as some foods have the power to lower the level of inflammation. Other foods have the power to increase it, and these are the foods that need to be drastically reduced, such as sugar, refined carbohydrates, and over-processed meats.

The benefits of this type of food plan are many. Among the most important: it reduces the risk of chronic diseases such as heart disease, cancer, gastritis, Crohn's disease and fibromyalgia. It improves cognitive functions, memory and attention, along with improving intestinal health. It provides the body with more energy and at the same time improves the quality of sleep; it also improves skin and hair health. And last but not least, it reduces and stabilizes body weight.

SYMPTOMS OF AN INFLAMED BODY

Symptoms of an inflamed body can be many; sometimes they have been with us for many years and we get used to it, but they can be defeated! Among the most common we can observe skin disorders, such as eczema, psoriasis or redness, muscle and joint stiffness, fatigue, anemia, irritability, difficulty sleeping or frequent awakenings during sleep, melancholy, inflamed gums and low fever in the evening.

STRATEGIES TO BEGIN A NEW LIFESTYLE

If you're starting a new diet, there are a few things you can do to set up your home and kitchen for success. First, take inventory of your pantry and refrigerator. Throw out any foods that aren't part of your new plan and stock up on healthy alternatives. So, get rid of any distractions that could lead you astray. This means getting rid of junk food from the house and making sure you have plenty of healthy snacks on hand. Finally, create a supportive environment by talking to your family and friends about your goals and asking for their help to stay on track. By following these simple steps, you will be well on your way to achieving your weight loss goals.

If you've decided to change your lifestyle and start eating healthier, there are a few things you can do to get started in the best way.

- Open your refrigerator and remove all the foods that will not be part of your new eating style. If you do not want to throw them away, donate them, but do not leave them at your disposal. It takes time to establish new habits and it is much better not to have junk food available. Stock up on healthy snacks, they will be very useful to you.

- One obstacle we can face when we decide to change is, incredibly, the family. Your family, your friends, they really love you, but they are used to knowing you as you are now. The early days will be a little shocking, especially if your change is radical. Calmly tell them that you have decided that you love yourself more and that you will appreciate their help and understanding. This does not mean a total change in your habits! It just means IMPROVEMENT. The tub of ice cream in front of the television or the chips will not be eliminated but simply replaced with REAL food that is much healthier. After some time, if you are constant, your body will recognize the 'right' foods from the 'wrong' ones and the old food will no longer be tempting. On the contrary, you will wonder how you managed to eat it for so many years.

- Get organized: equip your kitchen with everything you need, scales, non-stick pans, measuring cups, containers.

- Be flexible. Changing is never easy. If you make a mistake, if you fail sometimes … patience! Perfection is boring.

ALWAYS EMPHASIZE SEASONAL FRUITS AND VEGETABLES

TABLE OF SEASONAL FRUITS AND VEGETABLES

JANUARY

Vegetables: Beetroot, Broccoli, Artichokes, Carrots, Cauliflower, Cabbage, Chicory, Turnip greens, Beans, Fennel, Leeks, Radicchio, Celery, Pumpkin.

Fruit: Orange, Kiwi, Persimmon, Mandarins, Pomegranate, Apples, Pears.

FEBRUARY

Vegetables: Broccoli, Carrots, Cauliflower, Cabbage, Chicory, Fennel, Mushrooms, Radicchio, Celery, Spinach, Pumpkin.

Fruit: Oranges, Persimmons, Kiwi, Tangerine, Mandarin, Apples, Pears, Grapefruit.

MARCH

Vegetables: Dill, Asparagus, Broccoli, Thistle, Mushrooms, Lettuce, Peas, Radishes, Rocket, Celeriac, Celery, Spinach.

Fruit: Oranges, Bananas, Kiwi, Mandarin, Pears, Grapefruit, Avocado, Lemons.

APRIL

Vegetables: Asparagus, Beetroot, Broccoli, Artichokes, Carrots, Cauliflower, Cabbage, Chicory, Onions, Watercress, Beans, Broad Beans, Lettuce, Marjoram, Eggplant, New Potatoes, Peas, Turnips, Radishes, Rocket, Sage, Zucchini.

Fruit: Oranges, Avocado, Bananas, Strawberries, Kiwi, Lemons, Apple, Pears, Grapefruit.

MAY

Vegetables: Asparagus, Beets, Chard, Artichokes, Carrots, Cabbage, Chicory, Onions, Watercress, Beans, Green Beans, Broad Beans, Fennel, Lettuce, Marjoram, Eggplant, Potatoes, Peas, Tomatoes, Radicchio, Radishes, Rocket, Celery, Spinach, Zucchini.

Fruit: Oranges, Avocados, Cherries, Strawberries, Kiwis, Lemons, Apples, Pears, Grapefruit.

JUNE

Vegetables: Artichokes, Carrots, Cabbage, Cucumbers, Chicory, Green Beans, Broad Beans, Lettuce, Aubergines, Potatoes, Peppers, Peas, Tomatoes, Radicchio, Radishes, Rocket, Celery, Zucchini.

Fruit: Apricots, Bananas, Cherries, Strawberries, Kiwis, Lemons, Blueberries, Peaches, Plums.

JULY

Vegetables: Carrots, Onions, Cabbage, Cucumbers, Chicory, Green Beans, Broad Beans, Lettuce, Aubergines, Potatoes, Peppers, Tomatoes, Tomatoes, Radicchio, Radishes, Rocket, Celery, Zucchini.

Fruit: Apricots, Watermelons, Bananas, Cherries, Figs, Strawberries, Raspberries, Lemons, Melons, Blueberries, Peaches, Pears, Currants, Plums.

AUGUST

Vegetables: Carrots, Cabbage, Cucumbers, Chicory, Green Beans, Lettuce, Aubergines, Peppers, Potatoes, Tomatoes, Radicchio, Radishes, Rocket, Celery, Pumpkins, Zucchini.

Fruit: Apricots, Watermelons, Bananas, Cherries, Figs, Strawberries, Raspberries, Apples, Melons, Blueberries, Blackberries, Pears, Peaches, Plums, Currants, Grapes.

SEPTEMBER

Vegetables: Carrots, Cucumbers, Beans, Green Beans, Broad Beans, Mushrooms, Lettuce, Aubergines, New Potatoes, Peppers, Peas, Tomatoes, Rhubarb, Rocket, Celery, Zucchini, Celeriac.

Fruit: Apricots, Beetroot, Figs, Kiwi, Raspberries, Apples, Blackberries, Pears, Peaches, Plums, Grapes.

OCTOBER

Vegetables: Broccoli, Carrots, Brussels sprouts, Cabbage, Cauliflower, Cucumbers, Turnip greens, Mushrooms, Eggplants, Mint, Leeks, Celery, Truffles, Pumpkin, Zucchini.

Fruit: Peanuts, Bananas, Chestnuts, Prickly Pear, Kiwi, Pomegranate, Apples, Hazelnuts, Walnuts, Grapefruit, Pears, Grapes.

NOVEMBER

Vegetables: Broccoli, Artichokes, Carrots, Cauliflower, Brussels sprouts, Cabbage, Mushrooms, Endive, Aubergines, Radicchio, Celery, Spinach, Jerusalem artichokes, Truffles, Zucchini.

Fruit: Pineapple, Oranges, Avocado, Bananas, Chestnuts, Cedar, Mandarins, Pomegranate, Apples, Walnuts, Papaya, Pears, Grapefruit, Grapes.

DECEMBER

Vegetables: Broccoli, Artichokes, Cauliflower, Brussels sprouts, Cabbage, Turnip greens, Mushrooms, Endive, Olives, Radicchio, Celery, Spinach, Truffles.

Fruit: Pineapple, Oranges, Avocado, Bananas, Chestnuts, Mandarins, Kiwi, Mango, Apples, Pears, Grapefruit, Grapes.

LIST OF ANTI-INFLAMMATORY FOODS

INFLAMMATORY FOODS TO BE EATEN IN MODERATION
Farmed red meat, cured meats, cheeses, refined flours, sugar, gluten, coffee, alcohol, frying, fast food, industrial food.

ANTI-INFLAMMATORY FOODS
Whole grains and seeds, chia seeds, nuts, avocados, oats, quinoa, buckwheat, millet, red rice, seasonal vegetables and fruits, nuts, legumes, seaweed, berries, bearberry, blackcurrant, olive oil, coconut oil, avocado oil, salmon, organic eggs, extra dark chocolate, cinnamon, cayenne pepper, tomato.

FOODS WITH HIGH ANTI-INFLAMMATORY POTENTIAL
Amla berries, dog Rose, lemonade powder mix, pomegranate, ginseng, pecans with pellicle, walnuts with pellicle, brown rice, seaweed, soy sauce, pumpkin seeds, hemp seeds, flax seeds, onions, cauliflower, broccoli, turnips, daikon, radishes, rocket, ginger, turmeric, clove, cumin, tabasco, herbs, green mint, oregano, paprika, black pepper, peppermint, saffron, thyme, turmeric, wild marjoram, artichoke, kale, spinach, green tea, oily fish, oil hemp seeds, vitamin C, ginkgo biloba, grape seed extract.

NOTE: you'll notice that among the recipes in this book you won't see meat or chicken based recipes, except in rare occasions. This is because poultry and meat are highly inflammatory food and it's recommended to use them in moderation.

Breakfast

Morning Hazelnut Piadine

 Prep Time
10 min

 Cook Time
15 min

 Servings
4

- 1/2 cup of hazelnut flour
- 40 grams of sesame seeds
- 40 grams of ground flax seeds
- 2 tablespoons of psyllium powder
- 1 pinch of sea salt
- 1 teaspoon of turmeric
- 1 + 1/4 cup of warm water
- 1 tablespoon of coconut oil
- 1 dose of organic dry yeast powder

In a bowl, mix the hazelnut flour with the sesame seeds, ground flax seeds, psyllium, salt, turmeric and baking powder. In another bowl, mix the hot water well with the coconut oil. Gradually add the liquids to the other powdered foods and knead until a homogeneous mixture is obtained. Line a baking sheet with parchment paper, preheat the oven to 340° F. Roll out the dough and with the help of a large glass cut circles. Put the circles in the pan and cook for about 15/20 minutes. These wraps can be enjoyed with fresh fruit, vegetables or sauces.

Per serving: calories: 240 / fat: 22 / protein: 6 / carbs: 16

Muffin With Spinach And Cayenne Pepper

 Prep Time
15 min

 Cook Time
16 min

 Servings
6

- 800 grams of fresh spinach
- 2 organic egg whites naturally enriched with omega-3s
- 2 tablespoons of oat flour
- 2 tablespoons of olive oil
- 1 pinch of sea salt
- 1 teaspoon ground cayenne pepper

Cook the spinach in the steamer. If you do not have a steamer, boil the spinach in a pot of salted water for about 15 minutes, and drain very well. Put all the ingredients in a blender and blend until the mixture is well chopped but not creamy, use the pulse button. Fill the muffin tins and bake in a hot oven at 350° F for about 16/20 minutes.

Per serving: calories: 85 / fat: 3 / protein: 3 / carbs: 15 /

| Breakfast

Banana Pancakes With Apricots

 Prep Time
5 min

 Cook Time
10 min

 Servings
8

- 50 grams of banana flour
- 50 grams + 1 teaspoon of ghee
- 1 avocado
- 1 pinch of salt
- 1 teaspoon of turmeric powder
- 1 cup unsweetened coconut milk
- 5 pitted apricots

Combine the banana flour with the salt and turmeric powder. In another bowl, combine the 50 grams of ghee with the peeled and pitted avocado and mash with a fork. Combine the two preparations and add the coconut milk slowly, stirring constantly. Spread the dough with a ladle on a baking sheet covered with parchment paper, forming circles. Bake in a hot oven at 360° F for about 10 minutes. While the pancakes are cooking, cut the apricots into cubes and brown them for 5 minutes in a pan with a teaspoon of ghee. Serve pancakes with the apricot compote.

Per serving: calories: 129 / fat: 11 / protein: 1 / carbs: 10 /

Pudding With Blackcurrant And Mint

 Prep Time
3 minutes + 1 night rest

 Cook Time
5 min

 Servings
4

- 1 cup unsweetened coconut milk
- 2 tablespoons of ground Chia seeds
- 1 teaspoon of vanilla extract
- 1 pinch of salt
- 1 cup of blackcurrant
- 2 teaspoons of raw honey
- 5 fresh mint leaves
- 2 tablespoons of water

Combine the almond milk with the chia seeds, and add the vanilla extract and salt. Pour the mixture into small glasses and let it rest in the refrigerator overnight. In the morning mix the honey with the water and put in a non-stick pan with the currants, cook for 5 minutes. Pour the cooked currants over the puddings, which will have thickened overnight, decorate with mint leaves and enjoy.

Per serving: calories: 85 / fat: 3 / protein: 3 / carbs: 15 /

Anti inflammatory Diet Cookbook for Beginners 2022

Quinoa Bread With Pecan Walnut Butter

 Prep Time
15 minutes + 3 hours of rest

 Cook Time
30 min

 Servings
15

- 400 grams of pecan nuts with pellicle
- 200 grams of hazelnuts
- 6 drops of sage essential oil for food (or 1 tablespoon of sage powder)
- 500 grams of quinoa flour
- 1 dose of organic dry yeast
- 1 + 1/3 cup of water
- 2 tablespoons of olive oil

Place the pecans, hazelnuts, salt and sage essential oil in the blender, after having lightly toasted them in the oven at 350° F for 5 minutes. Continue to blend until the nuts begin to release their natural oil, blend until creamy, add water if necessary. Sage essential oil has a purifying power. If you don't have it, replace it with powdered sage.
The bread: mix the quinoa flour with the organic yeast and salt. Slowly add the oil and incorporate the water, preferably lukewarm, to the mixture. Work it with your hands until you get a smooth ball. Let it rise for at least 3 hours in a dark place, sheltered from drafts and warm. Bake in a hot oven at 360° F for about 30 minutes. This type of bread is very dry and crunchy, perfect for nut butter. Nut butter can be stored in an airtight food container in the refrigerator for at least a week.

Per serving: calories: 144 / fat: 4 / protein: 5 / carbs: 22 /

Oat Flakes With Pears And Blueberries

 Prep Time
3 min

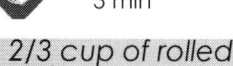 Cook Time
10 min

 Servings
2

- 2/3 cup of rolled oats
- 2 cups unsweetened almond milk
- 1 pinch of salt
- 1/4 cup of blueberries
- 1 pear
- 1 teaspoon of ground cinnamon
- 1 teaspoon of ground ginger
- 1 teaspoon of powdered mint

In a saucepan, bring the almond milk, salt, cinnamon, ginger and mint to a boil. Lower the heat to a minimum and add the oats, cook for about 10 minutes. Serve the oats with the fresh blueberries and pear. If you prefer a completely hot meal, heat the blueberries and pear in a teaspoon of ghee.

Per serving: calories: 166 / fat: 5 / protein: 5 / carbs: 27 /

| Breakfast

Soy Cream With Asparagus

 Prep Time 3 min   Cook Time 10 min   Servings 3

- 1 cup unsweetened natural soy yogurt
- 2 tablespoons of ground flaxseed
- 1 teaspoon of coconut oil
- 300 grams of asparagus
- 1 pinch of salt

Cook the asparagus in the steamer. If you do not have the steamer, boil the asparagus in a pan of lightly salted water for 10 minutes. Drain them well and cut them into small pieces. Put the yogurt in a bowl, add the ground flax seeds and mix well. Add the asparagus and season with the olive oil.

Per serving: calories: 156 / fat: 11 / protein: 8 / carbs: 10 /

Millet Cake With Plums

 Prep Time 10 min   Cook Time 30 min   Servings 10

- 2 cups of millet
- 4 cups of water
- 1 cup of rolled oats
- 10 pitted dried plums
- 2 fresh organic eggs
- 1 pinch of salt

Put the plums in a bowl of cold water and let them rest for 20 minutes. Cook the millet in 4 cups of water, add a pinch of salt and prunes. Remove from the heat and allow to cool, add the beaten eggs, mix carefully and bake in a preheated oven at 400° F for 30 minutes.

Per serving: calories: 100 / fat: 18 / protein: 3 / carbs: 18 /

Anti inflammatory Diet Cookbook for Beginners 2022 | 15

Pumpkin Sweet

 Prep Time
10 min

 Cook Time
20 min

 Servings
9

- 2 cups of banana flour
- 3 cups of diced pumpkin
- 3 Granny Smith apples
- 5 pitted plums
- 1/2 cup of blueberries
- 10 pitted dried plums
- 1 pinch of salt

Put the plums in a bowl of cold water and let them rest for 20 minutes. Cook the pumpkin in a non-stick pan with a teaspoon of olive oil, if necessary add water to finish cooking. Blend the pumpkin. Mix the plums cut into small pieces with their water, the pumpkin, the blueberries and the salt and banana flour. In an ovenproof dish lined with parchment paper, alternate a layer of pumpkin preparation with a layer of very thinly sliced apples. Bake in the oven at 400° F for about 20 minutes.

Per serving: calories: 129 / fat: 0 / protein: 11 / carbs: 33 /

Dried Fruit Breakfast Bars

 Prep Time
10 min

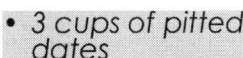 Cook Time
10 minutes + a night of rest

 Servings
14

- 3 cups of pitted dates
- 1 cup of pecans with pellicle
- 1/2 cup of rolled oats
- 3 tablespoons of ground flaxseed
- 2 teaspoons of raw cocoa powder
- 5 pitted plums
- 2 teaspoons of raw honey
- 1 pinch of salt
- 10 pitted dried plums
- 1 pinch of salt

Chop the dates and plums coarsely. Lightly toast the walnutsand blend them. Put them in a bowl and mix with the other ingredients. Roll out the dough into a baking sheet lined with parchment paper and let it rest in the refrigerator overnight. In the morning, remove the bars from the refrigerator and cut them into rectangles, bake the bars in the oven at 300° F for 10 minutes. These bars can be stored in the refrigerator in an airtight container for about 1 week.

Per serving: calories: 206 / fat: 6 / protein: 2 / carbs: 33 /

| Breakfast

Baskets Of Lentils And Carrots

 Prep Time 10 min   Cook Time 20 min   Servings 4

- 300 grams of lentils
- 1 organic egg
- 1 yellow onion
- 3 carrots
- 1 tablespoon of ground sage
- 1 pinch of salt
- 1 tablespoon of olive oil
- 1 pinch of cayenne pepper
- 1 pinch of salt
- 1 bay leaf

Cook the lentils in boiling water with the bay leaf. Chop the onion and put it in a non-stick pan with the oil and julienned carrots. Cook for 5 minutes, stirring, then add 4 tablespoons of water and salt, cover and finish cooking. Drain the lentils and add them to the beaten egg, sage and pepper. Spread the mixture into muffin tins and fill with carrots. cook at 350° F for about 20 minutes.

Per serving: calories: 162 / fat: 5 / protein: 12 / carbs: 17 /

Pudding Of Apricots And Hazelnuts

 Prep Time 15 min   Cook Time 10 min   Servings 6

- 1 cup of fresh apricots
- 90 grams of hazelnuts
- 1 +1/2 cup unsweetened coconut milk
- 1 teaspoon of vanilla extract
- 1 teaspoon of grated glass of organic lemon
- 1 pinch of salt
- 1 teaspoon of agar-agar powder

Remove the stone from the apricots and cut them into pieces. Put them in a pan with a pinch of salt and 1 tablespoon of water, cover and cook over very low heat, stirring occasionally. Chop the hazelnuts. In another saucepan, combine the hazelnuts with the apricots, the coconut milk and the rest of the ingredients. Bring the mixture to a boil, lower the heat, and cook for 5 minutes. Pour the pudding into glasses, allow to cool.

Per serving: calories: 181 / fat: 17 / protein: 3 / carbs: 7 /

Anti inflammatory Diet Cookbook for Beginners 2022 | 17

Brown Rice Cream

 Prep Time
10 min

 Cook Time
180 min

 Servings
3

- 1 cup of brown rice
- 1 pinch of salt
- 8 cups of water
- 1 teaspoon of vanilla extract
- 2 cups of strawberries
- 1 teaspoon of vanilla extract
- 1 teaspoon of raw honey

Wash the rice well and put it in a thick-bottomed pan, add the water and bring to a boil. Add the salt and set the heat to low. Cook for about 3 hours. Wash the strawberries and cut them into pieces, mix with the rice cream together with the other ingredients.

Per serving: calories: 92 / fat: 1 / protein: 2 / carbs: 21 /

Crepes Of Chickpeas And Spinach

 Prep Time
10 minutes + 2 hours of rest

 Cook Time
15 min

 Servings
4

- 1 cup of chickpea flour
- 1 cup of water
- 1 pinch of salt
- 2 tablespoons of olive oil
- 1 cup of spinach

In a non-stick pan cook the spinach with a tablespoon of olive oil, if necessary add a few tablespoons of water. Mix the chickpea flour with the water, salt and oil and leave to rest in the refrigerator for two hours. Heat a non-stick pan and grease with a little oil, pour a ladle of batter, the dough will be distributed, each ladle will be a crepe. Fill the crepes with spinach.

Per serving: calories: 121 / fat: 5 / protein: 6 / carbs: 14 /

| Breakfast

Frittata With Zucchini

 **Prep Time** 10 minutes + 1 hour rest

 **Cook Time** 10 min

 **Servings** 8

- 1 cup of chickpea flour
- 1 cup of water
- 1 pinch of salt
- 2 tablespoons of olive oil
- 1 cup of zucchini
- 1 red onion

Mix the chickpea flour with the water and let it rest in the refrigerator for 1 hour. Meanwhile, in a non-stick pan, cook the diced zucchini together with the chopped onion and oil. Mix the vegetables with the chickpea mixture and pour it into an ovenproof dish lined with baking paper. Cook at 400°F for about 20 minutes.

Per serving: calories: 165 / fat: 8 / protein: 6 / carbs: 17 /

Salads

Salad Of Fennel, Pecan Walnuts And Blueberries

 Prep Time
10 min

 Cook Time
10 min

 Servings
5

- 1/2 cup pecans with pellicle
- 1 cup of lentils
- 2 raw fennel
- 1 cup of blueberries
- 2 pitted figs
- 1 pinch of salt
- 2 tablespoons of olive oil
- 1 pinch of cayenne pepper
- 1 pinch of paprika
- 1 red onion

Toast the walnuts in a non-stick pan. Cook the lentils in plenty of lightly salted water and drain them very well, put them in a bowl. Add the crumbled walnuts, and the celery cut into very thin slices, the blueberries, the chopped figs, the onion cut into thin slices, the salt, the pepper and the paprika to the lentils. Mix well and serve.

Per serving: calories: 232 / fat: 13 / protein: 6 / carbs: 26 /

Eggplant And Pomegranate Salad

 Prep Time
10 min

 Cook Time
5 min

 Servings
5

- 2 eggplants
- 2 cups of peas
- 2 red onions
- 1 teaspoon of cilantro
- 1 pomegranate
- 1 pinch of salt
- 2 tablespoons of olive oil
- 1 pinch of cayenne pepper
- 80 grams of unsalted pistachios

Cut the aubergines into thin slices and grease them with very little oil with the help of a kitchen brush. In a non-stick pan, grill the aubergines on both sides without burning. Chop the cashewsBring a pot of water to a boil and cook the peas for 5 minutes, drain well. Chop the onions and sauté them in a lightly greased pot for 5 minutes. In a bowl put the aubergines cut into strips, the peas, the pomegranate seeds, the onion, the pistachios, the coriander, the pepper and the salt, mix well and serve.

Per serving: calories: 324 / fat: 14 / protein: 6 / carbs: 43 /

| Salads

Artichokes And Pears Salad

 Prep Time: 10 min

 Cook Time: 0 min

 Servings: 4

- 2 artichokes
- 2 brown pears
- 2 tablespoons of almonds
- 1 teaspoon of thyme
- 1 pinch of salt
- 2 tablespoons of olive oil
- 1 pinch of cayenne pepper

Clean the artichokes keeping the heart and remove the internal fluff. Cut the heart of the artichoke into very thin slices and put it in a bowl with a little lemon juice. Peel the pears and cut them into cubes. Chop the almonds. Drain the artichokes well and add them to the other ingredients.

Per serving: calories: 150 / fat: 9 / protein: 3 / carbs: 14 /

Rocket And Asparagus Salad

 Prep Time: 10 min

 Cook Time: 5 min

 Servings: 2

- 2 cups of rocket
- 2 cups of asparagus
- 2 tablespoons of walnuts
- 1 teaspoon of basil
- 1 pinch of salt
- 2 tablespoons of olive oil
- 1 pinch of cayenne pepper
- 1 clove of garlic

Chop the garlic and add it to the olive oil, pepper, salt and basil. Chop the walnuts. Steam the asparagus in lightly salted boiling water and cut them into small pieces. Combine all ingredients, mix well and serve.

Per serving: calories: 186 / fat: 17 / protein: 5 / carbs: 7 /

Fresh Summer Salad

 Prep Time
5 min

 Cook Time
0 min

 Servings
3

- 1 cup diced melon
- 1 cup diced cucumber
- 1 cup of lettuce
- 1 cup of celery
- 1 teaspoon of ground ginger
- 1 pinch of salt
- 2 tablespoons of olive oil
- 1 pinch of cayenne pepper
- 1 tablespoon of low sodium soy sauce

In a bowl, mix the soy sauce with the oil, salt, pepper and ginger. Cut the lettuce into strips, the celery into small pieces and combine with all the other ingredients, mixing well.

Per serving: calories: 117 / fat: 9 / protein: 1 / carbs: 7 /

Autumn Salad

 Prep Time
5 min

 Cook Time
0 min

Servings
3

- 1 cup of fresh baby spinach
- 1 cup of celery
- 2 shallots
- 1 teaspoon of fresh mint
- 1 pinch of salt
- 2 tablespoons of olive oil
- 1 pinch of cayenne pepper
- 1 unsweetened soy yogurt
- 1 pinch of saffron powder

In a bowl, mix the yogurt well with the finely chopped mint leaves, oil, salt, cayenne pepper and saffron. Chop the shallot, chop the celery. Combine all the ingredients in a bowl and mix carefully.

Per serving: calories: 141 / fat: 10 / protein: 5 / carbs: 8 /

| Salads

Exotic Salad

 Prep Time
5 min

 Cook Time
2 min

 Servings
3

- 1 cup of pineapple
- 1 cup of orange
- 1 shallot
- 1 tablespoon of pine nuts
- 1 pinch of salt
- 2 tablespoons of olive oil
- 1 pinch of cayenne pepper

Lightly toast the pine nuts in a non-stick pan, cut the pineapple into cubes, thinly slice the shallot. Peel and cut each orange wedge into three parts. Combine all the ingredients in a bowl and mix carefully.

Per serving: calories: 133 / fat: 7 / protein: 2 / carbs: 19 /

Salad With Red Cabbage

 Prep Time
10 min

 Cook Time
5 min

 Servings
6

- 1 cup of red cabbage
- 1 red onion
- 1 yellow onion
- 1 beetroot
- 5 pecans with pellicle
- 1 tablespoon of unsalted pistachios
- 2 tablespoons of olive oil
- 1 tablespoon of red wine vinegar
- 1 tablespoon of raw honey
- 1 pinch of cayenne pepper
- 1 spoonful of basil

Remove the outer leaves and the core of the cabbage and cut into very thin slices. boil the beetroot and make it into small cubes. Cut the onions into thin slices. chop the walnuts and pistachios. in a bowl, mix the oil well with the salt, pepper, chopped basil and honey. Combine all ingredients and mix carefully.

Per serving: calories: 133 / fat: 9 / protein: 1 / carbs: 9 /

Anti inflammatory Diet Cookbook for Beginners 2022 | 23

Fennel And Celery Salad

 Prep Time
5 min

 Cook Time
0 min

Servings
2

- 2 fennel
- 1 cup of celery
- 1 tablespoon of chervil
- 1 tablespoon of almonds
- 2 tablespoons of olive oil
- 1 pinch of cayenne pepper
- 1 pinch of salt
- the juice of an organic lemon

Clean the fennel, remove the outside and cut into very thin slices. Cut the celery into small pieces. Chop the almonds. In a bowl, mix the oil with the chopped chervil, pepper, lemon juice, salt. mix all ingredients carefully and serve.

Per serving: calories: 190 / fat: 15 / protein: 4 / carbs: 15 /

Salad Of Cucumbers And Soy Yogurt

 Prep Time
5 min

 Cook Time
0 min

Servings
4

- 2 cups of cucumbers
- 1 cup of leeks
- 1 tablespoon of chervil
- 8 Brazilian nuts
- 1 jar of unsweetened soy yogurt
- 2 tablespoons of olive oil
- 1 pinch of cayenne pepper
- 1 pinch of chili powder
- 1 pinch of salt

Peel the cucumbers and cut them into thin slices. Remove the external part and the final part of the leek and cut it into thin slices. chop the chervil along with the Brazil nuts. Add pepper, salt, oil and chili to the soy yogurt and mix carefully. Mix all the ingredients well.

Per serving: calories: 189 / fat: 14 / protein: 6 / carbs: 13 /

| Salads

Mixed Salad With Quinoa Bread

 Prep Time
7 min

 Cook Time
0 min

 Servings
4

- 1 tomato
- 1 leek
- 1 cucumber
- 1 tablespoon of pine nuts
- 2 slices of quinoa bread (see recipe)
- 1 tablespoon of fresh parsley
- 1 tablespoon of fresh basil
- 2 tablespoons of olive oil
- 1 pinch of black pepper
- 1 pinch of salt
- 1 teaspoon of turmeric
- 1 clove of garlic

Wash the tomato and slice. Remove the outer part and the final part of the leek and cut into slices. Peel the cucumber and cut it into cubes. Chop the basil with the parsley and the garlic. Mix the oil with the chopped herbs, turmeric, salt and pepper. Put the slices of bread cut into squares in a bowl, mix the vegetables with the flavored oil and pour all the ingredients on the bread.

Per serving: calories: 147 / fat: 5 / protein: 5 / carbs: 231 /

Greek Salad

 Prep Time
5 min

 Cook Time
0 min

 Servings
4

- 1 tomato
- 1 red pepper
- 1 cucumber
- 1 red onion
- 10 black olives
- 1 cup of boiled chickpeas
- 1 tablespoon of oregano
- 1 clove of garlic
- 2 tablespoons of olive oil
- 1 pinch of black pepper
- 1 pinch of salt

Wash the tomato and cut it into slices. Clean the pepper, cut it in half and remove the internal seeds, cut it into thin strips. Cut the cucumber into slices. Chop the onion. Combine all ingredients in a bowl and mix well.

Per serving: calories: 128 / fat: 5 / protein: 4 / carbs: 17 /

Anti inflammatory Diet Cookbook for Beginners 2022 | 25

Salad Of Celeriac

 Prep Time: 10 min
 Cook Time: 0 min
 Servings: 4

- 1 celeriac
- 1 celery
- 1 2 brown pears
- 1 red onion
- the juice of one lemon
- 1 cup pineapple
- 1 tablespoon of basil
- 2 tablespoons of olive oil
- 1 pinch of cayenne pepper
- 1 pinch of salt

Clean the celeriac and cut it into very thin slices. Remove the fibrous elements from the celery and cut it into slices. Peel and thinly slice the pears. Finely chop the basil and marinate it in olive oil for at least 30 minutes. Combine all the ingredients in a bowl and mix well.

Per serving: calories: 134 / fat: 7 / protein: 3 / carbs: 15 /

Radish And Hazelnut Salad

 Prep Time: 0 min
 Cook Time: 10 min
 Servings: 2

- 1 cup of radishes
- 1 leek
- 10 hazelnuts
- 1 tablespoon of sesame oil
- 1 tablespoon of thyme
- 1 tablespoon of sesame seeds
- 1 pinch of cayenne pepper
- 1 pinch of salt

Clean the celeriac and cut it into very thin slices. Remove the fibrous strands from the celery and cut it into slices. Peel and dice the pears. Combine all the ingredients in a bowl and mix well.

Per serving: calories: 109 / fat: 8 / protein: 3 / carbs: 9 /

| Salads

Salad Of Pastinaca And Red Beans

 Prep Time 10 min

 Cook Time 0 min

 Servings 2

- 2 parsnips
- 1 cup of boiled red kidney beans
- 1 tablespoon unsalted toasted pumpkin seeds
- 1 tablespoon of coconut oil
- 1 tablespoon of cilantro
- 1 pinch of cayenne pepper
- 1 pinch of salt

Clean the parsnips well, remove the skin and cut into thin slices. Combine with all the other ingredients in a bowl and mix well.

Per serving: calories: 103 / fat: 2 / protein: 5 / carbs: 12 /

Aromatic Salad

 Prep Time 10 min

 Cook Time 0 min

 Servings 2

- 1 bunch of fresh aromatic herbs
- 2 organic green Granny Smith apples
- 1 carrot
- 1 orange
- 1 tablespoon of hemp seeds
- 1 tablespoon of sesame oil
- the juice of one lemon
- 1 pinch of cayenne pepper
- 1 pinch of salt

Wash and chop all the aromatic herbs, put them in a bowl with the lemon juice, sesame oil, pepper, salt. Wash the apples very well and cut them into thin slices, without removing the peel. Peel the orange and divide each wedge into two parts. Julienne the carrot. Combine all ingredients in a bowl and mix well.

Per serving: calories: 98 / fat: 3 / protein: 2 / carbs: 18 /

Anti inflammatory Diet Cookbook for Beginners 2022 | 27

Goji Berry Salad

Prep Time 10 min

Cook Time 0 min

Servings 3

- 1/2 cup of goji berries
- 2 shallots
- 1 tomato
- 1 tablespoon of oregano
- 1 tablespoon of apple cider vinegar
- 1 cup of rocket
- 30 grams pistachios
- 1 tablespoon of olive oil
- 1 pinch of cayenne pepper
- 1 pinch of salt

Soak the goji berries in a cup of water for about half an hour. Meanwhile, chop the shallots and marinate them in a bowl with olive oil, lemon juice and vinegar. Slice the tomato and add it to the arugula and orange segments cut into small pieces. Add the goji berries and chopped pistachios.

Per serving: calories: 187 / fat: 9 / protein: 3 / carbs: 19 /

Spicy Salad

 **Prep Time** 10 min

 **Cook Time** 0 min

 Servings 3

- 2 carrots
- 2 red onions
- 1 red pepper
- 1 chili
- 1 tablespoon of cilantro
- 5 macadamia nuts
- 1 tablespoon of olive oil
- 1 pinch of cayenne pepper
- 1 pinch of salt

Julienne the carrots. Chop the onions. Divide the pepper into two parts, remove the internal seeds and cut into thin strips. Remove the seeds from the chili and chop it. Also chop the macadamia nuts. Put all the ingredients in a bowl and mix well.

Per serving: calories: 126 / fat: 8 / protein: 3 / carbs: 12 /

| Salads

Green Beans And Pine Nuts Salad

 **Prep Time** 10 min
 Cook Time 10 min
 Servings 4

- 1 cup of boiled green beans
- 1 grilled eggplant
- 2 tablespoons of ground flaxseed
- 1 tablespoon of pine nuts
- 1 pinch of salt
- 1 tablespoon of sesame oil
- 1 pinch of salt
- 1 pinch of cayenne pepper
- 5 fresh mint leaves

Wash the aubergine well, cut it into slices. Grease the slices on both sides with oil with the help of a kitchen brush and grill, without burning them, in a non-stick pan. Make them into strips. Cut the green beans into small pieces. Mix all the ingredients well and serve.

Per serving: calories: 103 / fat: 6 / protein: 4 / carbs: 10 /

Cucumber And Pomegranate Salad

 **Prep Time** 10 min
 Cook Time 0 min
 Servings 4

- 2 cups of cucumber
- 2 pomegranates
- 2 tomatoes
- 2 tablespoons of hemp seeds
- 1 tablespoon of pine nuts
- 6 leaves of dill
- 6 basil leaves
- 1 pinch of salt
- 2 tablespoons of olive oil
- 1 pinch of salt
- 1 pinch of cayenne pepper
- 5 fresh mint leaves
- 1 clove of garlic

Cut the cucumber into slices. Peel the pomegranates and remove the grains. Slice the tomatoes. Chop the garlic with the mint leaves, basil and dill. Mix all the ingredients together and serve.

Per serving: calories: 120 / fat: 9 / protein: 2 / carbs: 8 /

Soups

Spicy Pumpkin Soup

 Prep Time 10 min    Cook Time 45 min   Servings 5

- 2 cups of lentils
- 2 cups of squash
- 2 tomatoes
- 3 cups low sodium vegetable broth
- 2 red onions
- 6 leaves of dill
- 6 basil leaves
- 1 pinch of salt
- 2 tablespoons of olive oil
- 1 pinch of salt
- 1 pinch of cayenne pepper
- 1 chili
- 2 cloves of garlic

Cut the tomato into cubes, chop the onion with the chili. In a saucepan, fry the onion and add the tomato, cook for 5 minutes. Add the broth, lentils, salt, pepper and garlic, cook for 40 minutes. Coarsely chop the dill and basil leaves, add them to the soup and cook for the last 5 minutes. The soup can be eaten like this or pureed.

Per serving: calories: 133 / fat: 6 / protein: 6 / carbs: 17 /

Orange Soup

 Prep Time 12 min   Cook Time 45 min   Servings 4

- 2 cups of carrots
- 2 cups of squash
- 2 sweet potatoes
- 1 grated ginger root
- 2 cups of low sodium vegetable broth
- 1 cup unsweetened coconut milk
- 1 teaspoon of paprika
- 7 basil leaves
- 1 pinch of salt
- 2 tablespoons of olive oil
- 1 pinch of salt
- 1 pinch of cayenne pepper

Chop the basil leaves and put them in a pan with the oil and paprika. Dice the sweet potatoes, pumpkin and carrots and sauté for 5 minutes, stirring with a spoon. Add the broth and coconut milk, add the salt, pepper and ginger. Boil for 45 minutes over moderate heat. Serve hot.

Per serving: calories: 155 / fat: 8 / protein: 3 / carbs: 20 /

| Soups

Soup Of Black Beans And Zucchini

 Prep Time 15 min  Cook Time 45 min   Servings 4

- 2 cups of boiled black beans
- 1 cup of zucchini
- 2 cups of coconut water
- 2 cups unsweetened almond milk
- 2 cups low sodium vegetable broth
- 1 clove of garlic
- 1 teaspoon of chopped basil
- 1 tablespoon of cumin
- 1/2 cup unsweetened soy yogurt
- 1 pinch of salt
- 3 tablespoons of olive oil
- 1 pinch of salt
- 1 pinch of cayenne pepper

Put the oil in a saucepan, chop the garlic clove with the basil and cumin. Add the diced beans and courgettes and sauté for 5 minutes, always stirring with a fork. Add the broth, almond milk and coconut water, salt and pepper. Bring to a boil and then turn the heat down to low. Cook for 45 minutes. Put all the ingredients in the blender together with the soy yogurt and blend. Serve hot.

Per serving: calories: 270 / fat: 13 / protein: 10 / carbs: 31

Lentils And Turmeric Soup

 Prep Time 10 min   Cook Time 25 min   Servings 3

- 2 cups of boiled lentils
- 2 carrots
- 1 shallot
- 1 tablespoon of turmeric
- 1 cup unsweetened almond milk
- 1 cup low sodium vegetable broth
- 1 clove of garlic
- 1 teaspoon of parsley
- 1/2 cup unsweetened soy yogurt
- 1 pinch of salt
- 2 tablespoons of ghee
- 1 pinch of salt
- 1 pinch of cayenne pepper
- 1 tablespoon of sesame seeds

Wash and cut the carrots into pieces. Chop the shallot. Chop the garlic together with the parsley. Put the ghee in a saucepan and sauté the garlic and parsley for 1 minute. Add the lentils, carrots and sauté for 5 minutes. Add the cup of almond milk and the cup of broth, turmeric, salt and pepper and shallot. Cook over moderate heat for 25 minutes. Serve with the sesame seeds.

Per serving: calories: 249 / fat: 4 / protein: 16 / carbs: 41 /

Buckwheat Soup And Onions

 Prep Time
10 min

 Cook Time
20 min

Servings
3

- 2 cups of red onions
- 2 sweet potatoes
- 1/2 cup of buckwheat
- 1 shallot
- 1 tablespoon of thyme
- 2 cup unsweetened coconut milk
- 3 cup low sodium vegetable broth
- 1 clove of garlic
- 1 pinch of salt
- 3 tablespoons of olive oil
- 1 pinch of salt
- 1 pinch of cayenne pepper

Chop the garlic with the onions and the shallot. In a pan, brown the diced potatoes with the chopped onions and garlic for 5 minutes, adding the thyme. Add the coconut milk, salt and pepper, the vegetable broth and bring to a boil, add the buckwheat and cook over moderate heat for about 20 minutes. The soup can be enjoyed like this or pureed.

Per serving: calories: 389 / fat: 18 / protein: 8 / carbs: 49 /

Cauliflower And Tempeh Soup

 Prep Time
10 min

 Cook Time
25 min

 Servings
4

- 1 yellow onion
- 2 carrots
- 1 cauliflower
- 1 cup of Tempeh
- 1 tablespoon of cilantro
- 2 cup unsweetened hazelnut milk
- 3 cup low sodium vegetable broth
- 1 clove of garlic
- 1 pinch of salt
- 3 tablespoons of olive oil
- 1 pinch of salt
- 1 pinch of cayenne pepper
- 1 teaspoon of Tahina

Chop the onion with the carrot and garlic. Pour the oil into a pan and brown the chopped vegetables for 5 minutes. Add the cabbage cut into small pieces, coriander, salt, pepper, broth and hazelnut milk. Bring to a boil and cook over moderate heat for about 20 minutes. Add the diced tempeh, cook for another 5 minutes. Transfer the ingredients to the blender and blend together with the Tahina. Serve hot.

Per serving: calories: 249 / fat: 4 / protein: 7 / carbs: 39 /

| Soups

Broccoli And Brown Pear Soup

 Prep Time 10 min  Cook Time 25 min Servings 4

- 2 cups low sodium vegetable broth
- 1 cup of coconut water
- 2 red onions
- 2 cloves of garlic
- 2 sweet potatoes
- 1 teaspoon of tamari
- 3 brown pears
- 600 grams of broccoli
- 1 pinch of salt
- 2 tablespoons of olive oil
- 1 pinch of cayenne pepper
- 1 tablespoon of sesame seeds

Cut the onions into slices; peel and cut the potatoes into cubes. Bring the broth and coconut water to a boil in a saucepan, pour in the onions, potatoes, garlic, oil, broccoli, salt, pepper and diced pears. Lower the heat to low and cook for about 25 minutes. Transfer to the blender and blend until pureed. Serve hot with the sesame seeds and Tamari.

Per serving: calories: 223 / fat: 8 / protein: 7 / carbs: 29 /

Saffron Artichokes Soup

 Prep Time 10 min Cook Time 20 min Servings 4

- 2 cups low sodium vegetable broth
- 1 cup unsweetened almond milk
- 8 artichokes
- 2 cups of boiled cannellini beans
- 1 sachet of saffron
- 1 pinch of salt
- 2 tablespoons of olive oil
- 1 pinch of cayenne pepper
- 1 tablespoon of pine nuts

Clean the artichokes by removing the outer leaves and the fluff inside. Cut them into pieces. Bring the vegetable broth and almond milk to a boil in a saucepan. Pour in the artichokes, cannellini beans, salt, oil and pepper. Cover and set on moderate heat, cook for about 20 minutes. Transfer to the mixer, add the saffron and blend until a thick cream is obtained. Serve with the pine nuts.

Per serving: calories: 252 / fat: 7 / protein: 14 / carbs: 41 /

Chestnut And Bean Soup

 Prep Time: 5 min
Cook Time: 25 min
Servings: 3

- 2 cups low sodium vegetable broth
- 1 cup unsweetened hazelnut milk
- 2 cups of boiled green beans
- 1 yellow onion
- 160 grams of boiled chestnuts
- 1 teaspoon of rosemary
- 1 pinch of salt
- 2 tablespoons of coconut oil
- 1 pinch of cayenne pepper
- 10 hazelnuts

Boil the chestnuts and remove the peel and chop. Chop the onion and rosemary and brown them in a saucepan with the coconut oil. Add the boiled and chopped green beans, add salt and pepper. Cook for 5 minutes, stirring with a ladle, add the chestnuts, hazelnut milk, broth and cook over medium heat for about 20 minutes. Serve the soup hot with the chopped hazelnuts.

Per serving: calories: 184 / fat: 6 / protein: 5 / carbs: 28 /

Turnip And Spelled Soup

Prep Time: 10 min
Cook Time: 25 min
Servings: 3

- 3 cups low sodium vegetable broth
- 1 cup of unsweetened soy milk
- 600 grams of turnip
- 1 red onion
- 1 cup of spelled
- 1 teaspoon of thyme
- 1 pinch of salt
- 2 tablespoons of olive oil
- 1 pinch of cayenne pepper
- 1 teaspoon of turmeric

Chop the onion and brown it in the olive oil together with the thyme. Add the diced turnip, salt and pepper. Add the cup of soy and half cup of vegetable stock, cover and cook for 15 minutes over moderate heat. In another saucepan, bring the remaining vegetable broth with the turmeric to a boil and cook the spelled for about 20 minutes. Blend the turnip, drain the farro well and mix. Serve the creamy soup hot.

Per serving: calories: 199 / fat: 14 / protein: 7 / carbs: 17 /

| Soups

Topinambur And Potato Soup

 Prep Time: 10 min
 Cook Time: 30 min
 Servings: 4

- 600 grams of Jerusalem artichoke
- 1 tablespoon of Italian seasoning
- 2 sweet potatoes
- 1 shallot
- 5 cups low sodium vegetable broth
- 1 clove of garlic
- 2 tablespoons of olive oil
- 1 pinch of cayenne pepper
- 10 pecans with pellicle

Clean the Jerusalem artichokes and cut them into cubes; peel the potatoes and cut them. Chop the shallot and brown it for 5 minutes in the olive oil in a saucepan. Add the broth, Jerusalem artichoke, potatoes, salt, pepper. Cook over medium heat for about 30 minutes. Transfer to the blender and blend until pureed. Serve the soup hot with the chopped pecans.

Per serving: calories: 291 / fat: 9 / protein: 12 / carbs: 48 /

Spinach And Kale Soup

 Prep Time: 5 min
 Cook Time: 30 min
Servings: 4

- 3 cups of spinach
- 3 cups of kale
- 1 sweet potato
- 1 yellow onion
- 4 cups low sodium vegetable broth
- 1 cup of unsweetened soy milk
- 2 tablespoons of olive oil
- 1 pinch of cayenne pepper
- 2 tablespoons of hemp seeds

Bring the vegetable broth and soy milk to a boil, add the spinach, kale, peeled and diced sweet potato, salt and pepper. Cook over medium heat for about 30 minutes. Transfer to a mixer and blend well. Serve hot with the hemp seeds.

Per serving: calories: 153 / fat: 11 / protein: 6 / carbs: 12 /

Spinach And Broccoli Soup

 Prep Time: 5 min Cook Time: 60 min Servings: 3

- 1 cup of oats
- 4 cups low sodium vegetable broth
- 1 cup of broccoli
- 1 cup of spinach
- 1 onion
- 1 clove of garlic
- 1 tablespoon of parsley
- 2 tablespoons of olive oil
- 1 pinch of cayenne pepper
- 10 almonds

Bring a pot of lightly salted water to a boil and cook the oats for about 35 minutes. Check the cooking times on the package to be sure, they change slightly according to the type of brand. Once cooked, drain well. Chop the onion with the garlic and parsley and brown in the olive oil for 5 minutes. Add the broccoli and spinach, salt and pepper and finally the broth. Cook over medium heat for about 25 minutes. Transfer to a blender and add the oats; blend until a thick cream is obtained. Serve with the chopped almonds.

Per serving: calories: 201 / fat: 9 / protein: 7 / carbs: 27 /

Bean Soup And Lemon

 Prep Time: 5 min Cook Time: 15 min Servings: 4

- 2 cups of fresh broad beans
- 1 shallot
- 1 tablespoon of coconut butter
- 2 cups low sodium vegetable broth
- 1/2 cup unsweetened soy yogurt
- 1 tablespoon of Italian seasoning
- the zest of an organic lemon
- 1 pinch of black pepper
- 1 pinch of salt

Bring a pan of lightly salted water to a boil and cook the beans for about 10 minutes. In a bowl, mix the yogurt well with the Italian seasoning. Chop the shallot and fry it for 5 minutes in coconut butter, add the well-drained broad beans and the vegetable broth, bring to the boil and transfer to a blender. Add the lemon zest and blend until creamy. Serve with the yogurt dressing.

Per serving: calories: 174 / fat: 6 / protein: 6 / carbs: 23 /

| Soups

Pearl Barley And Red Beans Soup

Prep Time: 5 min
Cook Time: 25 min
Servings: 6

- 1 cup of Brussels sprouts
- 1 cup of boiled red kidney beans
- 1/2 cup boiled red lentils
- 5 cups low sodium vegetable broth
- 1 cup of pearl barley
- 1 tablespoon of thyme
- 1 tablespoon of turmeric
- 1 pinch of black pepper
- 1 pinch of salt

Soak the Brussels sprouts in a bowl of cold water with a tablespoon of coarse salt for 10 minutes. After this time, remove the outer leaves and cut the sprouts into quarters. Bring the vegetable broth to a boil and add the sprouts, beans, lentils and pearl barley, salt and pepper. Cook over medium heat for about 25 minutes. Transfer to a mixer together with the thyme and blend until puree is obtained.

Per serving: calories: 129 / fat: 1 / protein: 7 / carbs: 20 /

Soup Of Mushrooms And Tempeh

Prep Time: 5 min
Cook Time: 25 min
Servings: 3

- 600 grams of cremini mushrooms
- 1/2 cup of tempeh
- 2 yellow onions
- 5 cups low sodium vegetable broth
- 3 tablespoons of rice flour
- 1 tablespoon of parsley
- 1 pinch of black pepper
- 1 pinch of salt
- 2 tablespoons of olive oil

Clean the mushrooms and cut them. Put the olive oil in a saucepan with the chopped onions and parsley and brown them for 5 minutes. Add the vegetable broth, the diced tempeh and cook for about 25 minutes. Add the rice flour and mix for 5 minutes. Transfer all the ingredients to a mixer and blend until creamy.

Per serving: calories: 206 / fat: 13 / protein: 13 / carbs: 15 /

Cauliflower And Miso Soup

Prep Time: 5 min
Cook Time: 30 min
Servings: 3

- 1 cauliflower
- 1 tablespoon of Miso
- 2 yellow onions
- 2 carrots
- 5 cups low sodium vegetable broth
- 1 tablespoon of parsley
- 1 pinch of black pepper
- 1 pinch of salt
- 2 tablespoons of coconut oil

In a saucepan, sauté the chopped onions for 5 minutes, add the chopped cabbage and the chopped carrots, cook for 5 minutes, stirring with a cooking spoon. Add the vegetable stock, salt, pepper and parsley. Cook over moderate heat for about 25 minutes, add the miso and cook for another minute. Transfer all the ingredients to a mixer and blend until creamy.

Per serving: calories: 183 / fat: 4 / protein: 9 / carbs: 33 /

Asparagus And Tamari Soup

Prep Time: 5 min
Cook Time: 25 min
Servings: 2

- 2 sweet potatoes
- 1 cup of asparagus
- 2 tablespoons of Tamari
- 3 cups low sodium vegetable broth
- 1 cup of coconut water
- 1 tablespoon of basil
- 1 pinch of black pepper
- 1 pinch of salt
- 1 tablespoon of olive oil

Peel and cut the potatoes into cubes, clean the asparagus and cut them into small pieces. Put the vegetable broth and coconut water in a saucepan, bring to a boil and add the potatoes, asparagus, salt, pepper, olive oil, basil and cook over medium heat for about 25 minutes. Transfer to the food processor and blend until creamy. Season with the tamari and serve hot.

Per serving: calories: 228 / fat: 8 / protein: 6 / carbs: 37 /

| Soups

Spinach And Corn Flour Soup

Prep Time: 5 min
Cook Time: 10 min
Servings: 3

- 4 cups of fresh spinach
- 1/2 cup of cornmeal
- 5 cups low sodium vegetable broth
- 1 carrot
- 1 red onion
- 1 teaspoon of paprika
- 1 pinch of cayenne pepper
- 1 pinch of salt
- 2 tablespoons of olive oil

In a saucepan, sauté the chopped onion and carrot in the olive oil for 3 minutes, then add the vegetable broth, salt, pepper and spinach and bring to the boil. Cook over medium heat for 5 minutes and add the cornmeal very slowly, stirring constantly. When the cornmeal has thickened, the soup will be ready.

Per serving: calories: 230 / fat: 9 / protein: 6 / carbs: 33 /

Pomegranate And Pistachio Soup

Prep Time: 5 min
Cook Time: 30 min
Servings: 3

- 4 sweet potatoes
- 2 pomegranates
- the zest of an organic lemon
- 20 grams of unsalted pistachios
- 1 red onion
- 5 cups low sodium vegetable broth
- 1 pinch of cayenne pepper
- 1 pinch of salt
- 2 tablespoons of olive oil

In a saucepan, sauté the chopped onion for 5 minutes. Add the vegetable broth and bring to a boil. Peel the potatoes and dice them, add them to the broth together with the salt, pepper and a tablespoon of olive oil and cook over medium heat for about 25 minutes. Put the pomegranate seeds, lemon zest and a tablespoon of oil in a bowl, mix and set aside. Transfer the potatoes to the blender and blend well. Serve the soup hot with the chopped pistachios and the flavored pomegranate seeds.

Per serving: calories: 265 / fat: 12 / protein: 4 / carbs: 32 /

Pasta & Cereals

Basmati Rice With Peppers

Prep Time 5 min | **Cook Time** 35 min | **Servings** 2

- 1 cup of basmati rice
- 1 red pepper
- 1 yellow pepper
- 1/2 cup of green beans
- 1 tablespoon of cilantro
- 1 red onion
- 1 pinch of cayenne pepper
- 1 pinch of salt
- 2 tablespoons of olive oil

In a saucepan with plenty of lightly salted water, boil the rice for about 15 minutes. Clean the peppers, cut them in half and remove the seeds inside. Chop the onion with the cilantro. In a large pan, fry the onion and coriander for 5 minutes in the olive oil, add the chopped peppers and chopped green beans and cook over medium heat for about 20 minutes, if necessary add a few tablespoons of vegetable broth to finish cooking. Drain the rice well and add it to the peppers, mix with the salt and pepper and serve.

Per serving: calories: 299 / fat: 14 / protein: 5 / carbs: 40 /

Buckwheat With Broccoli, Zucchini And Aubergines

Prep Time 10 min | **Cook Time** 30 min | **Servings** 2

- 1 cup of buckwheat
- 2 courgettes
- 1/2 cup of broccoli
- 1 eggplant
- 5 pecans with pellicle
- 1 pinch of cayenne pepper
- 1 pinch of salt
- 2 tablespoons of olive oil
- chopped walnuts

In a saucepan with plenty of lightly salted water, boil the buckwheat for about 15 minutes, drain and season with a tablespoon of olive oil. In a pan, heat the remaining oil slightly, add the diced aubergine and cook for 5 minutes, stirring, then add the broccoli and chopped courgettes. Add the salt and pepper and finish cooking the vegetables. Combine the vegetables with the cooked buckwheat and add the chopped walnuts.

Per serving: calories: 274 / fat: 11 / protein: 9 / carbs: 41 /

Wholemeal Pasta With Tofu, Pine Nuts And Leek

Prep Time 10 min **Cook Time** 15 min **Servings** 5

- 320 grams of wholemeal pasta
- 1 cup of leeks
- 200 grams of tofu
- 2 tablespoons of pine nuts
- 1/4 cup vegetable broth
- 1 tablespoon of basil
- 1 pinch of cayenne pepper
- 1 pinch of salt
- 2 tablespoons of olive oil

Coarsely blend the tofu in the mixer with the pulse button. In a pan, lightly heat a tablespoon of oil and brown the tofu with the basil. Add the leeks cut into rings, salt and pepper and cook them with the broth until soft. In a saucepan, bring abundant salted water to the boil and cook the pasta for the cooking time indicated on the package. Drain the pasta and sauté it in a pan with the leeks, add the pine nuts and raw oil and serve.

Per serving: calories: 313 / fat: 10 / protein: 13 / carbs: 36 /

Quinoa With Figs And Peppers

Prep Time 10 min **Cook Time** 5 min **Servings** 2

- 1 cup of quinoa
- 2 red peppers
- 6 figs
- 1 tablespoon of Italian seasoning
- 1/4 cup vegetable broth
- 1 pinch of cayenne pepper
- 1 pinch of salt
- 1 sachet of saffron
- 2 tablespoons of olive oil

Bring plenty of salted water to a boil and cook the quinoa for 15 minutes. Dissolve the saffron in the vegetable broth. In a pan, lightly heat the olive oil and add the peppers cleaned and without the internal seeds tangled into small pieces, and the figs cut into small pieces. Brown for 5 minutes with Italian seasoning and cook them with the saffron-flavored broth until soft. Drain the quinoa well and season with the peppers and saffron figs.

Per serving: calories: 272 / fat: 9 / protein: 8 / carbs: 38 /

Anti inflammatory Diet Cookbook for Beginners 2022

Wholemeal Spaghetti With Cod And Parsley And Garlic Sauce

Prep Time: 5 min
Cook Time: 20 min
Servings: 5

- 320 grams of wholemeal spaghetti
- 200 grams of cod
- 1/2 cup unsweetened soy yogurt
- 1 tablespoon of parsley
- 2 cloves of garlic
- the juice of half a lemon
- 1 pinch of cayenne pepper
- 1 pinch of salt
- 2 tablespoons of olive oil

Bring plenty of lightly salted water to a boil in a saucepan and cook the whole spaghetti according to the cooking times indicated on the package. Chop the garlic and parsley. In a pan, lightly heat the olive oil and cook the diced cod for 10 minutes, add salt and pepper. In a bowl, mix well the soy yogurt with the chopped parsley and garlic and the lemon juice. Drain the spaghetti and toss with the yogurt sauce and cod.

Per serving: calories: 288 / fat: 7 / protein: 18 / carbs: 37 /

Barley Tomatoes, Capers And Anchovies

Prep Time: 5 min
Cook Time: 25 min
Servings: 2

- 1 cup of barley
- 2 tomatoes
- 2 cloves of garlic
- 8 anchovies in oil
- 1 tablespoon of capers
- 1 teaspoon of red pepper
- 1 pinch of cayenne pepper
- 1 pinch of salt
- 2 tablespoons of olive oil

Chop the chili with garlic and brown it in a pan with olive oil. Add the anchovies well drained from the oil, the diced tomatoes, the salt and pepper, the capers and cook for 5 minutes over medium heat. Bring plenty of lightly salted water to a boil in a saucepan and cook the barley for about 20 minutes. Drain the barley well and dress it with the sauce.

Per serving: calories: 270 / fat: 14 / protein: 3 / carbs: 0 /

| Pasta & Cereals

Barley, Olives And Tofu

Prep Time: 10 min
Cook Time: 15 min
Servings: 3

- 1 cup of barley
- 2 tomatoes
- 2 cloves of garlic
- 1 red onion
- 1 cucumber
- 6 pitted black olives
- 200 grams of natural Tofu
- 1 pinch of cayenne pepper
- 1 pinch of salt
- 2 tablespoons of olive oil

Bring plenty of lightly salted water to a boil in a saucepan, and when it boils, add the barley and cook for about 15 minutes. Wash and cut the tomatoes into cubes, cut the onion into thin slices, peel and slice the cucumber. Cut the tofu into cubes and chop it, put it in a pan with the oil and cook for 3 minutes. Add the well-drained barley, olives, tomatoes, cucumber, salt and pepper, onion and minced garlic, mix well and cook for 1 minute, stirring.

Per serving: calories: 276 / fat: 17 / protein: 12 / carbs: 26 /

Wholemeal Pasta With Avocado And Apple

Prep Time: 5 min
Cook Time: 15 min
Servings: 4

- 200 grams of wholemeal pasta
- 1 green Granny Smith apple
- 1 tablespoon of parsley
- 1 avocado
- 20 grams of pine nuts
- the juice of half a lemon
- 1 pinch of cayenne pepper
- 1 pinch of salt
- 2 tablespoons of olive oil

Bring plenty of lightly salted water to a boil in a saucepan and cook the quinoa for 15 minutes. Wash the parsley, peel and cut the avocado. In a blender, blend the avocado with the parsley, a tablespoon of olive oil, the lemon juice, the salt and the pepper. In a pan, lightly heat a tablespoon of olive oil and add the well-drained quinoa. Cut the apple into thin slices, add it to the quinoa, add the avocado cream and mix. Decorate with pine nuts and serve.

Per serving: calories: 346 / fat: 17 / protein: 8 / carbs: 41 /

Buckwheat Gnocchi With Salmon And Shrimps

Prep Time: 5 min
Cook Time: 20 min
Servings: 15

- 300 grams of buckwheat flour
- 1 cup of water
- 1 teaspoon of salt
- 200 grams of peeled and boiled shrimp
- 200 grams of wild salmon
- 1 cup of rocket
- 1 pinch of cayenne pepper
- 1 pinch of salt
- 2 tablespoons of olive oil

Heat the cup of water with the teaspoon of salt, dissolve the salt well. Slowly add the buckwheat flour and mix. When the dough has thickened, transfer it to a work surface and continue to knead with your hands. When it is blended, form cylinders as thick as a finger and cut them into small pieces forming the gnocchi. In a pan, heat a tablespoon of olive oil and brown the shrimps for a few minutes with the salt and pepper. Transfer them to a bowl and add the chopped rocket and chopped salmon. Bring abundant salted water to a boil in a saucepan, pour in the gnocchi and, as soon as the water boils and the gnocchi rise to the surface, drain. Combine the gnocchi with the salmon and shrimp, mix and serve with a tablespoon of raw oil.

Per serving: calories: 382 / fat: 10 / protein: 28 / carbs: 43 /

Millet With Tuna And Broccoli

Prep Time: 10 min
Cook Time: 30 min
Servings: 3

- 1 cup of millet
- 2 cups of broccoli
- 200 grams of tuna in water
- 2 cloves of garlic
- 2 tablespoons of parsley
- 10 hazelnuts
- 1 pinch of cayenne pepper
- 1 pinch of salt
- 2 tablespoons of olive oil

Bring plenty of lightly salted boiling water to a boil and cook the millet for about 15 minutes. In a pan heat the olive oil and brown the chopped parsley and garlic for 5 minutes. Add the broccoli and tuna, salt, pepper and cook for about 10 minutes. Drain the millet and toss with the broccoli and tuna, add the chopped hazelnuts and serve.

Per serving: calories: 257 / fat: 14 / protein: 17 / carbs: 18 /

| Pasta & Cereals

Wholemeal Pasta And Shiitake Mushrooms

Prep Time: 30 min
Cook Time: 20 min
Servings: 6

- 400 grams of wholemeal pasta
- 1 cup of peas
- 6 dried shiitake mushrooms
- 2 shallots
- 2 bay leaves
- 1 pinch of black pepper
- 1 pinch of salt
- 2 tablespoons of olive oil

Soak the mushrooms in water for 30 minutes. After this time, drain them and set the water aside. In a pan heat the olive oil, add the chopped shallot, chopped mushrooms, peas, salt and pepper and sauté for 5 minutes. Add the filtered mushroom water, cover and cook for 15 minutes over moderate heat. Bring plenty of lightly salted water to a boil, when it boils, add the pasta and bay leaves, cook according to the cooking times indicated on the package. Drain the pasta and remove the bay leaves. Pour the pasta into the pan with the mushrooms and peas, toss, stirring for a minute and serve.

Per serving: calories: 384 / fat: 7 / protein: 8 / carbs: 69 /

Rice With Aubergines And Octopus

Prep Time: 10 min
Cook Time: 60 min
Servings: 4

- 1 cup of brown rice
- 600 grams of octopus
- 2 eggplants
- 1 tomato
- 1 tablespoon of parsley
- 1 clove of garlic
- 1 teaspoon of curry
- 1 pinch of black pepper
- 1 pinch of salt
- 2 tablespoons of olive oil

Bring plenty of lightly salted water to a boil and cook the octopus for 25 to 30 minutes. Wash and cut the aubergines and tomato into cubes. Chop the garlic and parsley, put them in a pan with the olive oil and brown with the vegetables for 5 minutes, add 4 tablespoons of boiling water and the curry. Mix and cover and cook over moderate heat for another 10 minutes. Drain the octopus well and put it in a bowl with the vegetables, mix well. Cook the rice in abundant salted water for 15 to 20 minutes, drain and season with the octopus and vegetable sauce.

Per serving: calories: 297 / fat: 9 / protein: 34 / carbs: 26 /

Baked Wholemeal Pasta Gratin

Prep Time: 10 min
Cook Time: 20 min
Servings: 4

- 400 grams of wholemeal pasta
- 1 cup of tomato puree
- 2 cloves of garlic
- 1/2 cup chopped parsley
- 2 tablespoons of nutritional yeast
- 1 tablespoon of dried chili
- 1 pinch of black pepper
- 1 pinch of salt
- 2 tablespoons of olive oil

Bring plenty of salted water to a boil and cook the pasta for half the cooking time indicated on the package. In a saucepan, lightly heat the olive oil and add the tomato sauce together with 2 tablespoons of water and cook for 10 minutes. Drain the pasta and put it in a bowl. Combine the pasta with the tomato sauce, chopped parsley, chopped garlic, chili and mix well. Line an oven dish with parchment paper, add the dough and cover with the nutritional yest. Bake in a hot oven at 370° F for 10 minutes, check that the pasta is cooked and serve.

Per serving: calories: 257 / fat: 8 / protein: 5 / carbs: 28 /

Kamut With Green Beans And Saffron Mushrooms

Prep Time: 5 min
Cook Time: 40 min
Servings: 4

- 300 grams of kamut
- 200 grams of boiled green beans
- 200 grams of white mushrooms
- 2 cloves of garlic
- 1/2 cup chopped parsley
- 1 sachet of dried saffron
- 1 pinch of black pepper
- 1 pinch of salt
- 2 tablespoons of olive oil
- 30 grams of unsalted pumpkin seeds

In a pan of lightly salted boiling water, cook the kamut for about 25 minutes. Heat the oil in a pan and add the chopped green beans and the sliced mushrooms, add the salt, pepper, and chopped parsley and garlic. Cook for 10 minutes, stirring constantly, add the saffron, mix and set aside. Drain the kamut well, sauté it for 5 minutes in a pan with the mushrooms and green beans and add the pumpkin seeds. Serve hot.

Per serving: calories: 223 / fat: 14 / protein: 22 / carbs: 94 /

| Pasta & Cereals

Bulgur With Edamame Beans And Sprouts

Prep Time: 5 min
Cook Time: 30 min
Servings: 3

- 1 cup of bulgur
- 1 cup of boiled edamame beans
- 200 grams of bean sprouts
- 2 yellow onions
- 1 tablespoon of chopped basil
- 1 pinch of salt
- 1 pinch of cayenne pepper
- 2 tablespoons of olive oil
- 1 tablespoon of low sodium soy sauce
- pumpkin seeds

Cook the bulgur for about 15 minutes in plenty of lightly salted boiling water. Chop the onions and brown them in a non-stick pan with olive oil for 3 minutes. Add the beans, salt, pepper and soy sauce, mix and cook for 10 minutes. Add the bean sprouts and continue cooking for 5 minutes. Drain the bulgur well, toss it in the vegetable pan and serve with the pumpkin seeds.

Per serving: calories: 215 / fat: 11 / protein: 10 / carbs: 19 /

Rice With Chicken And Broccoli (To eat occasionally)

Prep Time: 5 min
Cook Time: 40 min
Servings: 6

- 2 cups of brown rice
- 200 grams of lean, skinless chicken
- 1 cup of broccoli
- 2 carrots
- 1 leek
- 1 tablespoon of Italian seasoning
- 20 grams of almonds
- 1 pinch of salt
- 1 pinch of cayenne pepper
- 2 tablespoons of olive oil
- 1 tablespoon of Tamari

Cook the rice for about 25 minutes in plenty of salted water. Cut the chicken breast into cubes. Clean the leek and carrots and chop them. In a non-stick pan, lightly heat the olive oil and brown the chopped carrots and leek for 5 minutes. Add the chicken, salt and pepper and continue cooking for 10 minutes, adding a few tablespoons of water if necessary. Drain the rice, add the almonds, season with the Tamari and mix well. Serve hot.

Per serving: calories: 168 / fat: 7 / protein: 12 / carbs: 14 /

Venus Rice With Mackerel And Tomatoes

Prep Time 5 min
Cook Time 35 min
Servings 5

- 2 cups of black rice
- 200 grams of mackerel in oil
- 1 cup of cherry tomatoes
- 2 courgettes
- 1 tablespoon of parsley
- 1 tablespoon of chopped mint leaves
- 1 clove of garlic
- 1 chili
- 1 pinch of salt
- 1 pinch of cayenne pepper
- 2 tablespoons of olive oil

Bring plenty of salted water to a boil and cook the Venere rice for 20-25 minutes. In the meantime, chop the parsley with mint, garlic and chili and brown them in a non-stick pan with the olive oil for 5 minutes, stirring constantly. Add the well-drained mackerel from the oil and the diced cherry tomatoes and the courgettes cut into very thin slices. Cook for 5 minutes. Drain the rice well and sauté it in a pan with the fish and cherry tomatoes, serve hot.

Per serving: calories: 240 / fat: 12 / protein: 13 / carbs: 20

Wholemeal Spaghetti With Pears, Cashews And Asparagus

Prep Time 10 min
Cook Time 20 min
Servings 5

- 400 grams of wholemeal spaghetti
- 300 grams of asparagus
- 1 cup of cherry tomatoes
- 2 brown pears
- 15 unsalted cashews
- 1/2 cup unsweetened soy yogurt
- 1 tablespoon of basil
- 1 tablespoon of parsley
- 1 pinch of salt
- 1 pinch of cayenne pepper
- 2 tablespoons of olive oil
- the juice of half a lemon

Clean the asparagus and cook them in a steamer. If you do not have a steamer, cook them in lightly salted water for 15 minutes, drain and cut them into pieces. In a non-stick pan, lightly heat the olive oil and add the chopped parsley and diced tomatoes, salt and pepper and cook for 5-7 minutes, add the asparagus and cook for a couple of minutes. Put the soy yogurt in a bowl and add the chopped basil and cashews. Peel the pears and cut them into very small cubes and season with the lemon juice. Cook the spaghetti in plenty of lightly salted water for the cooking time indicated on the package, drain and place in a bowl with the asparagus and cherry tomato sauce, the nacardi sauce and the lemon pears. Mix well and serve hot.

Per serving: calories: 245 / fat: 8 / protein: 7 / carbs: 36 /

| Pasta & Cereals

Quinoa With Totani Dried Tomatoes And Chickpeas

Prep Time: 5 min
Cook Time: 30 min
Servings: 7

- 2 cups of quinoa
- 10 dried tomatoes in oil
- 1 cup of boiled chickpeas
- 400 grams of squid rings
- 1 red onion
- 1 tablespoon of parsley
- 1 pinch of salt
- 1 pinch of cayenne pepper
- 2 tablespoons of olive oil

Cook the quinoa for about 15 minutes in plenty of lightly salted water. In a non-stick pan heat the olive oil and brown the squid rings with the chopped parsley and onion, salt, pepper and dried tomatoes drained from the oil and chopped. Cook for about 10 minutes, stirring with a spoon. Drain the quinoa well and toss in a pan with the squid, add the boiled chickpeas, mix and serve hot.

Per serving: calories: 298 / fat: 8 / protein: 15 / carbs: 45 /

Pasta With Anchovies, Broccoli And Pecan Nuts

Prep Time: 5 min
Cook Time: 30 min
Servings: 4

- 200 grams of pasta
- 1 cup of broccoli
- 200 grams of anchovies in oil
- 10 pecans
- 1 shallot
- 1 tablespoon of basil
- 1 pinch of salt
- 1 pinch of cayenne pepper
- 2 tablespoons of olive oil

In a non-stick pan, lightly heat the olive oil, chop the walnuts with the shallot and basil and brown for 1 minute. Add the broccoli and cook for 10 minutes, stirring constantly. If necessary, add a couple of tablespoons of boiling water to finish cooking. Add salt, pepper, and after 10 minutes add the chopped anchovies, and cook for another minute. Cook the pasta in lightly salted boiling water for the cooking time indicated on the package, drain and dress it with the anchovy and broccoli sauce.

Per serving: calories: 251 / fat: 15 / protein: 13 / carbs: 16 /

Anti inflammatory Diet Cookbook for Beginners 2022

Farro With Zucchini, Tuna And Leek

Prep Time: 5 min
Cook Time: 25 min
Servings: 7

- 2 cups of farro
- 3 courgettes
- 200 grams of tuna in water
- 1/2 cup boiled peas
- 1 white onion
- 1 tablespoon of parsley
- 1 pinch of salt
- 1 pinch of cayenne pepper
- 2 tablespoons of olive oil

Cook the farro in plenty of lightly salted water for 25-30 minutes. In a non-stick pan, lightly heat the olive oil and add the chopped parsley and onion and leek. Cook for 1 minute and add the boiled peas, the tuna, and the washed and julienned courgettes. Cook for 10 minutes mixing often, add salt and pepper. Drain the spelled well and mix with the tuna, serve hot.

Per serving: calories: 268 / fat: 4 / protein: 16 / carbs: 45 /

Wholemeal Rice With Pumpkin, Ghee And Nuts

Prep Time: 5 min
Cook Time: 25 min
Servings: 3

- 1 cup of brown rice
- 1 cup diced squash
- 1 tablespoon of ghee
- 1/4 cup chopped walnuts
- 1 white onion
- 1 tablespoon of parsley
- 1 cup low sodium vegetable broth
- 1 pinch of salt
- 1 pinch of cayenne pepper
- 2 tablespoons of olive oil

In a non-stick pan, heat the olive oil slightly and add the chopped onion and parsley. Cook for about 2 minutes and add the diced pumpkin, salt and pepper, brown for 5 minutes and add the broth, cook over medium heat until the pumpkin becomes soft. Cook the rice in plenty of lightly salted water according to the cooking time indicated on the package, drain well and add it to the pumpkin mix with the ghee. Serve with chopped walnuts.

Per serving: calories: 196 / fat: 13 / protein: 3 / carbs: 17 /

| Pasta & Cereals

Wholemeal Pasta With Walnut Pesto, Pecan Basil And Dried Tomatoes

Prep Time: 5 min
Cook Time: 20 min
Servings: 3

- 200 grams of wholemeal pasta
- 15 dried cherry tomatoes
- 10 pecans with pellicle
- 1 cup of fresh basil
- 1 teaspoon of oregano
- 1 pinch of salt
- 1 pinch of cayenne pepper
- 3 tablespoons of olive oil

Put the pecans, 2 tablespoons of olive oil, the basil, the dried tomatoes drained from the oil, the pepper in the food processor and blend well until you get a smooth cream. Cook the pasta in plenty of lightly salted water for the time indicated on the package, drain it well and mix it with the pesto, oregano and a tablespoon of raw oil. Serve hot.

Per serving: calories: 279 / fat: 14 / protein: 8 / carbs: 33 /

Wholemeal Pasta With Zucchini Flowers, Tomatoes, Anchovies And Pine Nuts

Prep Time: 5 min
Cook Time: 15 min
Servings: 4

- 250 grams of wholemeal pasta
- 10 dried cherry tomatoes
- 2 tablespoons of pine nuts
- 1 tablespoon of parsley
- 200 grams of zucchini flowers
- 10 anchovies in oil
- 1 pinch of salt
- 1 pinch of cayenne pepper
- 3 tablespoons of olive oil

In a non-stick pan heat the olive oil slightly and brown the parsley with the dried tomatoes drained from the oil and chopped for 3 minutes, add the chopped anchovies and cook for a couple of minutes. Now add the courgette flowers and cook for another 5 minutes. In a saucepan, bring plenty of lightly salted water to a boil and cook the wholemeal pasta for the cooking time indicated on the package, drain it and put it in a pan with the sauce. Serve hot.

Per serving: calories: 313 / fat: 15 / protein: 6 / carbs: 31 /

Spicy Quinoa Cauliflower And Almonds

Prep Time: 5 min
Cook Time: 20 min
Servings: 4

- 1 cup of quinoa
- 1 cup of cauliflower
- 20 grams of almonds
- 1 chili
- 1 clove of garlic
- 10 fresh mint leaves
- 1 pinch of salt
- 1 pinch of cayenne pepper
- 2 tablespoons of olive oil

Cook the quinoa for about 15 minutes in plenty of lightly salted boiling water. Chop together the mint leaves, chili and garlic. Chop the almonds separately. In another pan, cook the cauliflower in boiling water flavored with lemon juice until it becomes soft. Transfer the cauliflower to a mixer and blend until smooth. Drain the quinoa and add the cauliflower cream, the chopped almonds and the aromatic herbs, add salt and pepper and the raw oil.

Per serving: calories: 254 / fat: 12 / protein: 8 / carbs: 30 /

| Pasta & Cereals

Vegetarians

Sweet Potatoes In Sweet And Sour Sauce

Prep Time: 5 min
Cook Time: 20 min
Servings: 3

- 2 tablespoons of coconut oil
- 3 sweet potatoes
- 1 clove of garlic
- 1 chili
- 1 white onion
- 1 tablespoon of cilantro
- 1 pinch of salt
- 3 tablespoons of low sodium soy sauce
- 3 tablespoons of red wine vinegar
- 1 teaspoon of coconut sugar or alternatively 1 tablespoon of yacon syrup
- 1 tablespoon of rice flour

In a bowl, mix well the yacon syrup, soy sauce, vinegar and rice flour. In a non-stick pan, lightly heat a tablespoon of coconut oil and brown the peeled and diced potatoes for 5 minutes, add a couple of tablespoons of boiling water and continue cooking until soft. Set them aside. In another pan put the other spoonful of coconut oil and fry the chopped onion and garlic for 5 minutes. Add the potatoes, mix and add the sauce. Cook for a couple of minutes over moderate heat. Mix with the chopped cilantro and chili. Serve hot.

Per serving: calories: 156 / fat: 3 / protein: 3 / carbs: 30 /

Salt Cake With Asparagus And Mushroom Cream

Prep Time: 20 min
Cook Time: 40 min
Servings: 8

- 2 cups of asparagus
- 500 grams of cremini mushrooms
- 1 tablespoon of Italian seasoning
- 1 tablespoon of olive oil
- 1 tablespoon of coconut butter
- 200 grams of buckwheat flour
- 100 grams of rice flour
- 4 tablespoons of sesame oil

Clean the asparagus and boil them in lightly salted water for 10 minutes, then drain and cut them into small pieces. Put the coconut butter in a non-stick pan and brown the asparagus for 5 minutes, add salt and pepper. In another pan put the mushrooms with the olive oil and the Italian seasoning and cook them for about 15 minutes; if necessary complete the cooking by adding a few tablespoons of warm water. In a bowl combine a pinch of salt, buckwheat flour and rice flour and mix well. Add the sesame oil and 1/2 cup of slightly warm water and knead. If necessary, add more water, a little at a time. Roll out the dough with a rolling pin and transfer it to an ovenproof dish lined with baking paper. Blend the mushrooms in a blender and spread the cream obtained over the dough and bake in a hot oven at 350° F for about 30 minutes. Remove the dish from the oven, add the asparagus and bake again for 5 minutes.

Per serving: calories: 206 / fat: 7 / protein: 7 / carbs: 32 /

Rice Paper Rolls With Broccoli And Tofu

Prep Time: 30 min
Cook Time: 10 min
Servings: 10

- 10 rice paper wrappers
- 3 cups of broccoli
- 300 grams of Greek feta
- 5 dried cherry tomatoes
- 1 tablespoon of sesame seeds
- 2 tablespoons of black olive pate
- 1 tablespoon of olive oil
- a pinch of salt

In a pot of lightly salted boiling water, cook the broccoli for about 10 minutes, drain very well and put them in a bowl. Chop the dried tomatoes and add them to the broccoli, then add the salt, pepper, sesame seeds, olive pate and coarsely crumbled feta. Mix everything with a fork. Wet a rice waffle by immersing it for a few moments in a bowl of cold water. Place it on the work surface and stuff it in the center with the vegetables, then wrap the rice paper on itself. Repeat the process with all the rolls. Arrange the rice paper wrappers on a serving tray and serve.

Per serving: calories: 135 / fat: 9 / protein: 5 / carbs: 10 /

Quenelle Of Cannellini Beans With Hummus And Parsley Cream

Prep Time: 25 min
Cook Time: 40 min
Servings: 6

- 300 grams of boiled cannellini beans
- 4 tablespoons flax seeds
- 1 teaspoon of cilantro
- 1 pinch of salt
- 1 cup of boiled chickpeas
- 1 tablespoon of olive oil
- the juice of half a lemon
- 1 tablespoon of Tahina
- 1 pinch of cayenne pepper
- 1 bunch of fresh parsley
- 1 cup unsweetened soy yoghurt
- 1 tablespoon of coconut oil

Put the cannellini beans boiled with the flax seeds, a pinch of salt, a pinch of pepper, the coriander and the olive oil in a blender, blend until the mixture is smooth. With two spoons form quenelles, alternatively moisten your hands with cold water and form round meatballs. Arrange the meatballs on a baking tray lined with parchment paper and season with a little olive oil. Cook at 370° F for about 30-35 minutes. Leave them to cool after cooking in order to make them more compact. While the meatballs are cooling, prepare the hummus and the parsley cream. Put the parsley, yogurt, a pinch of salt and the coconut oil in a blender, blend well and set aside. Put the chickpeas, lemon juice, Tahina, a pinch of salt and pepper in the blender, blend until you reach the desired consistency. Serve the quenelles with the two sauces.

Per serving: calories: 271 / fat: 6 / protein: 14 / carbs: 37 /

| Vegetarians

Zucchini Fritters With Garlic Sauce

Prep Time: 30 min
Cook Time: 15 min
Servings: 4

- 5 courgettes
- 2 organic eggs
- 3 tablespoons of rice flour
- 2 tablespoons of nutritional yeast
- 1 cup unsweetened coconut yogurt
- 3 tablespoons of grated quinoa bread (see recipe)
- 8 fresh mint leaves
- 2 cloves of garlic
- 3 tablespoons of olive oil
- 1 pinch of black pepper
- 1 pinch of salt

Put the yogurt in a colander with a bowl underneath and put it in the refrigerator for 30 minutes. After this time, the yogurt will have eliminated the excess water; season it with a pinch of salt and minced garlic and put it back in the refrigerator. Wash the courgettes and cut them into julienne strips, beat the eggs and add them to the courgettes, breadcrumbs, nutritional yest, salt and pepper and chopped mint. In a non-stick pan, lightly heat the olive oil and cook the pancakes by spoonfuls, turning them to brown on both sides. Serve the fritters hot with the coconut sauce.

Per serving: calories: 238 / fat: 16 / protein: 7 / carbs: 13 /

White Onions Filled With Rice

Prep Time: 25 min
Cook Time: 35 min
Servings: 4

- 4 large white onions
- 1/2 cup of basmati rice
- 1 tablespoon of capers
- 1 tablespoon of mixed aromatic herbs to taste
- 1 pinch of salt
- 1 pinch of pepper
- 3 tablespoons of olive oil

Bring plenty of lightly salted water to a boil in a saucepan and cook the rice for about 15 minutes, drain well. Remove the outer layer of the onions and cook them for about 3 minutes in boiling water, drain and let them cool. Cut off the top and empty the inside with a kitchen spoon. Heat a tablespoon of olive oil in a non-stick pan and brown the inside of the onions removed with a spoon, add salt and pepper, add a tablespoon of boiling water and cook until the onions are soft. Combine the onions with the rice, the chopped capers, the chopped aromatic herbs and mix. Fill the onions with the rice mixture, line a baking sheet with parchment paper and bake in a preheated oven at 400° F for about 35 minutes. Serve seasoned with raw olive oil.

Per serving: calories: 176 / fat: 11 / protein: 3 / carbs: 20 /

Tempeh With Ginger Sauce

Prep Time: 10 min
Cook Time: 25 min
Servings: 4

- 300 grams of tempeh
- 2 tablespoons of sesame oil
- 1 ginger root
- 200 grams of Chinese cabbage
- 1/2 cup low sodium vegetable broth
- 1 tablespoon of rice vinegar
- 1 teaspoon of chili powder
- 1 pinch of salt
- 2 tablespoons of low sodium soy sauce
- 1 tablespoon of maple syrup

Cut the tempeh into cubes. In a bowl, mix the soy sauce with the maple syrup and a tablespoon of grated ginger root, mix well and add the tempeh. Leave to marinate for 20 minutes. Heat the sesame oil in a non-stick pan and brown the remaining thinly sliced ginger, add the diced cabbage and cook until soft, adding the vegetable broth to finish cooking. Place the cabbage in a bowl and pan where it was cooked. Remove the tempeh quickly, leaving aside the marinade. Combine the cabbage tempeh with the chopped chili pepper and season with the marinade.

Per serving: calories: 159 / fat: 9 / protein: 15 / carbs: 22 /

Sweet Potato Carpaccio With Cremini Mushroom Cream

Prep Time: 10 min
Cook Time: 20 min
Servings: 4

- 600 grams of cremini mushrooms
- 3 sweet potatoes
- 2 tablespoons of olive oil
- 3 tablespoons of grated quinoa bread (see recipe)
- 1 tablespoon of oregano
- 1 tablespoon of almond butter
- 1 pinch of salt
- 1 pinch of cayenne pepper

Peel the potatoes into very thin slices and put them in a bowl with cold water for 10 minutes. After this time, boil the potato slices for one minute in boiling water, drain and let them dry. line a baking sheet with parchment paper, distribute the potatoes and with a kitchen brush grease them with coconut oil mixed with oregano, add salt and pepper and crumbled bread. Brown them in the oven for 3 minutes with the oven grill function. In a non-stick pan, lightly heat the olive oil and cook the mushrooms until soft, add a pinch of salt, if necessary add a few tablespoons of water to finish cooking. Place the mushrooms in a food processor and blend until smooth. Serve the potatoes with the cream on top.

Per serving: calories: 203 / fat: 9 / protein: 4 / carbs: 28 /

| Vegetarians

Spinach With Leek And Hazelnuts

Prep Time: 10 min | **Cook Time:** 15 min | **Servings:** 2

- 2 tablespoons of coconut oil
- 2 leeks
- 10 hazelnuts
- 1 clove of garlic
- 1 pinch of nutmeg
- 1 tablespoon of wine vinegar
- 2 cups of spinach
- 1 pinch of salt
- 1 pinch of cayenne pepper

Chop the garlic and brown it lightly in a non-stick pan with coconut oil, add the sliced leeks and cook over moderate heat until soft. Add the hazelnuts, vinegar and a pinch of nutmeg. In a saucepan, bring plenty of lightly salted water to a boil and cook the spinach for 15 minutes, drain very well and add to the leeks, mix. Serve hot.

Per serving: calories: 105 / fat: 9 / protein: 3 / carbs: 6 /

Algae Chips

Prep Time: 5 min | **Cook Time:** 5 min | **Servings:** 2

- 10 sheets of Nori seaweed
- 1 pinch of salt
- 1 tablespoon of sesame seeds
- 2 tablespoons of sesame oil
- 1 pinch of chili powder

Wet the seaweed with water from the shiniest part with the help of a kitchen brush. In a bowl, mix the sesame oil, the chili pepper, the salt and the sesame seeds. Line a baking sheet with parchment paper, distribute the seaweed and with a kitchen brush, grease them with the prepared sesame oil. Bake in the oven for 5 minutes at 300° F. Allow to cool and break into small pieces.

Per serving: calories: 61 / fat: 5 / protein: 4 / carbs: 4 /

Greek Feta With Tomatoes And Almond Pesto

Prep Time: 5 min
Cook Time: 0 min
Servings: 3

- 200 grams of feta
- 1 tablespoon of nutritional yeast
- 4 tablespoons of chopped basil
- 10 almonds
- 1 clove of garlic
- 3 tablespoons of olive oil
- 10 cherry tomatoes
- 5 pitted black olives

Put the basil, the almonds, a pinch of salt, the nutritional yeast and 2 tablespoons of olive oil in a blender. Blend until creamy. Cut the feta cheese into cubes, add the pesto, the cherry tomatoes cut in half and the olives, mix well and serve.

Per serving: calories: 341 / fat: 31 / protein: 12 / carbs: 7 /

Artichokes And Beet Frittata

Prep Time: 5 min
Cook Time: 10 min
Servings: 7

- 8 organic eggs
- 1 cup of artichoke hearts in oil
- 1 beetroot
- 1 tablespoon of cilantro
- 2 tablespoons of olive oil
- 1 pinch of salt
- 1 pinch of cayenne pepper

Boil the beetroot in boiling water until soft, drain and cut into cubes. Put the artichokes in a colander and drain the oil well. Beat the eggs, add the salt, pepper, coriander, artichokes and beetroot. Grease a non-stick pan with olive oil, heat slightly and pour in the preparation. Cook for 5 minutes on each side.

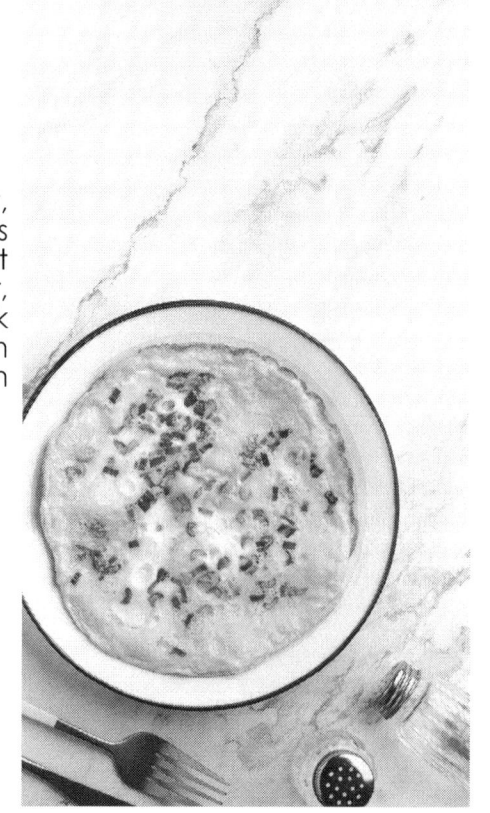

Per serving: calories: 141 / fat: 4 / protein: 8 / carbs: 4 /

| Vegetarians

Potato Croquettes With Pumpkin Seeds

Prep Time: 5 minutes + 20 of rest
Cook Time: 15 min
Servings: 6

- 400 grams of rice flour
- 1 teaspoon of dried sage
- 1 organic egg
- 3 cups unsweetened almond milk
- olive oil for frying
- 3 yellow potatoes
- 200 grams of ricotta cheese
- 2 tablespoons of pumpkin seeds
- 1 pinch of salt
- 1 pinch of black pepper

Mix the flour with the sage and a pinch of salt. Beat the eggs with the milk, add them to the flour and mix, let it rest in the refrigerator for 20 minutes. Heat a tablespoon of oil in a non-stick pan and brown the potatoes made in small cubes for 5 minutes. Add a few tablespoons of boiling water and cook until they become soft, transfer them to a bowl. Add the ricotta, the pumpkin seeds and the egg and milk batter, mix well. Heat the olive oil in a pan and cook the mixture in spoonfuls for 3 minutes, then turn over to the other side and cook another 3 minutes. Serve hot.

Per serving: calories: 236 / fat: 6 / protein: 9 / carbs: 37 /

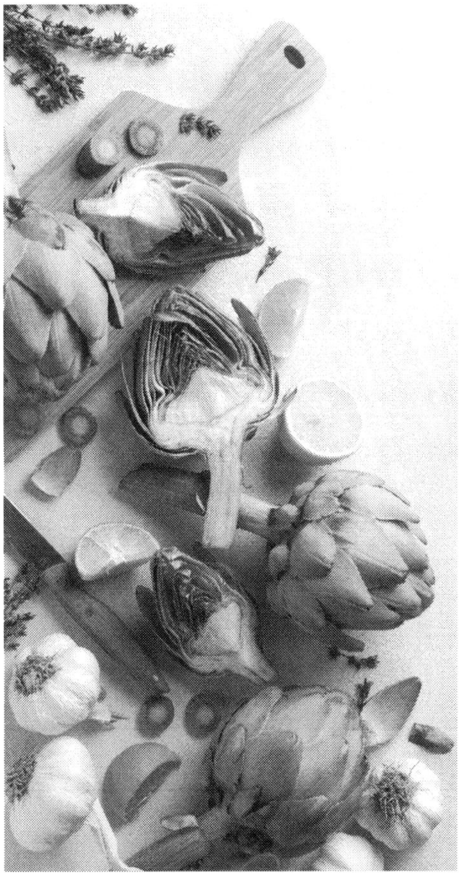

Artichokes Flan

Prep Time: 5 min
Cook Time: 30 min
Servings: 3

- 2 cups of artichoke hearts in oil
- 2 cups of unsweetened soy milk
- 2 organic eggs
- 1 tablespoon of nutritional yeast
- 1 tablespoon of coconut butter
- 1 pinch of salt
- 1 pinch of black pepper

Drain the excess oil from the artichokes. Put the artichokes in a pan with the milk, salt, pepper and bring to a boil, cook for 10-15 minutes. Transfer to a blender and blend together with the eggs, a pinch of salt, a pinch of pepper and the nutritional yeast. Pour the mixture into a greased pan with the coconut butter and bake at 350° F for about 20 minutes.

Per serving: calories: 215 / fat: 11 / protein: 12 / carbs: 17 /

Tempeh With Olives And Capers

Prep Time: 5 min
Cook Time: 8 min
Servings: 3

- 600 grams of tempeh
- 2 tablespoons of black olives
- 2 chopped shallots
- 2 teaspoons of paprika
- 2 tablespoons of olive oil
- 1 pinch of salt
- 1 pinch of cayenne pepper

In a non-stick pan, lightly heat the olive oil and brown the shallots for 5 minutes. Add the diced tempeh, paprika and chopped olives. Add the salt and pepper and cook for 3 minutes, stirring.

Per serving: calories: 317 / fat: 18 / protein: 29 / carbs: 43 /

Rolls Of Quinoa Lettuce And Raspberries

Prep Time: 15 min
Cook Time: 15 min
Servings: 3

- 200 grams of quinoa
- 1 head of lettuce
- 1 cucumber
- 10 cherry tomatoes
- 1 tablespoon of chopped fresh mint leaves
- 2 tablespoons of raspberries
- 1 organic lemon
- 3 tablespoons of olive oil
- 3 tablespoons of cottage cheese
- 1 pinch of salt
- 1 pinch of cayenne pepper

Cook the quinoa in plenty of lightly salted water for about 15 minutes, drain well. Remove the larger leaves from the lettuce without breaking them and wash them. Peel the cucumber and cut it into thin slices. Wash the cherry tomatoes and cut them into four parts. Put the raspberries in a blender with the mint, lemon juice and olive oil and blend well. Mix the quinoa with the cucumber, cherry tomatoes, cheese and raspberry sauce. Spread the quinoa filling in the center of the salad leaves, and close with a toothpick.

Per serving: calories: 310 / fat: 14 / protein: 10 / carbs: 39

| Vegetarians

Pastinache With Broccoli Cream

Prep Time: 10 min
Cook Time: 30 min
Servings: 3

- 6 parsnips
- 2 cups of broccoli
- 10 pecans with pellicle
- 100 grams of ricotta cheese
- 1/2 cup unsweetened soy milk
- 1 teaspoon of turmeric
- 1 tablespoon of olive oil
- 1 pinch of salt
- 1 pinch of black pepper

Clean and cut the parsnips into cubes, cook them in plenty of lightly salted boiling water for about 15 minutes and drain well. In another saucepan, bring the water to a boil and cook the broccoli for 10 minutes. In a non-stick pan, heat the olive oil and brown the parsnips for 5 minutes, adding the salt and pepper. Put the broccoli in a blender along with the turmeric, soy milk, cheese, pecans and blend well. In a bowl, mix the mixture with the parsnips and serve.

Per serving: calories: 223 / fat: 13 / protein: 7 / carbs: 21 /

Chutney Of Red Onions, Turnip And Apples

Prep Time: 10 min
Cook Time: 45 min
Servings: 10

- 3 cups of boiled diced beetroot
- 3 red onions
- 2 ripe apples
- 2 tablespoons of maple syrup
- 5 tablespoons of apple cider vinegar
- 2 tablespoons of grated ginger root
- 1 pinch of salt

Place the boiled and diced turnips in a thick-bottomed pot. Chop the onions. Peel the apples and cut them into cubes. Add the apples, syrup, onions, ginger, salt and vinegar to the turnips and cook over very low heat for 45 minutes, mixing very often. Allow to cool and place in a hermetically sealed glass container.

Per serving: calories: 64 / fat: 0 / protein: 1 / carbs: 15 /

Hamburger Of Black Rice & Chickpeas

Prep Time: 10 min
Cook Time: 30 min
Servings: 6

- 1 cup of boiled chickpeas
- 1 cup of kale
- 1 cup of black rice
- 1 tablespoon of chopped fresh basil
- 2 tablespoons of olive oil
- 1 pinch of salt
- 1 pinch of cayenne pepper
- 1 red onion
- 3 tablespoons of corn flour

Cook the black rice in a pan of lightly salted boiling water for about 20 minutes, drain well. In a bowl, mash the chickpeas with a fork, add a tablespoon of olive oil, the chopped basil, salt and pepper. In a non-stick pan heat a tablespoon of olive oil and brown the chopped kale, cook until soft, adding a few tablespoons of boiling water if necessary. Combine the kale with the chickpeas and rice and mix everything. Form the hamburgers with your hands and flour them on both sides with the corn flour. Cook the burgers in olive oil for 3 minutes on each side and serve with raw onion rings.

Per serving: calories: 230 / fat: 7 / protein: 8 / carbs: 36 /

Piadine With Tofu And Berries

Prep Time: 15 min
Cook Time: 35 min
Servings: 6

- 100 grams of wholemeal flour
- 100 grams of banana flour
- 100 grams of buckwheat flour
- 5 tablespoons of olive oil
- 1/2 cup unsweetened coconut milk
- 1/2 cup of coconut water
- 1 pinch of salt
- 1 teaspoon of baking soda
- 1 tablespoon of chopped fresh mint leaves
- 200 grams of tofu
- 1 tablespoon of goji berries
- 1 tablespoon of grated ginger
- 1/2 cup diced melon
- 1/2 cup of blueberries
- 1/2 cup unsweetened soy yogurt

In a bowl, mix the flours with the salt and baking soda. Slowly add the coconut milk, the coconut water and mix well. Shape into a ball and let it rest in the refrigerator for a couple of hours. Meanwhile, crumble the tofu with your hands and mix it with the ginger, the goji berries (soaked in water for 20 minutes and drained), the melon, the chopped mint, the yogurt and the blueberries. Remove the dough from the refrigerator and divide it into six parts, shape into balls and roll them out with a rolling pin. Cook the wraps in a non-stick pan lightly greased with oil, a minute or two on each side. Fill the wraps with the filling and serve.

Per serving: calories: 303 / fat: 15 / protein: 7 / carbs: 38 /

| Vegetarians

Vegan

Pasta With Chestnut Ragout

Prep Time: 10 min
Cook Time: 25 min
Servings: 8

- 600 grams of wholemeal pasta
- 200 grams of boiled chestnuts
- 250 of natural seitan
- 3 tomatoes
- 2 carrots
- 1 red onion
- 2 stalks of celery
- 1 tablespoon of chopped fresh basil
- 4 tablespoons of olive oil

Chop the onion, carrot and celery and brown them in the oil for 5 minutes. Coarsely chop the chestnuts and seitan and add them to the vegetables. Cook for 2 minutes and add the diced tomatoes, add salt and pepper, continue cooking for 15 minutes over moderate heat. Bring a pan of lightly salted water to a boil and cook the pasta for the cooking time indicated on the package. Drain it and season with the ragout and basil.

Per serving: calories: 296 / fat: 8 / protein: 12 / carbs: 26 /

Curry Pastinache Cream With Leek And Black Beans

Prep Time: 10 min
Cook Time: 30 min
Servings: 4

- 500 grams of parsnips
- 3 cups low sodium vegetable broth
- 2 leeks
- 200 grams of boiled black beans
- 2 tablespoons of olive oil
- 1 teaspoon of Italian seasoning
- 1 teaspoon of saffron powder
- 1 pinch of cayenne pepper
- 1 pinch of salt

Peel the pastinache and make them into cubes. Brown them for 5 minutes in a non-stick pan with the olive oil, add the vegetable broth, saffron, Italian seasoning and cook for about 25 minutes. Wash the leek and cut it into slices. Brown it in a non-stick pan with a tablespoon of olive oil for 3 minutes, add the beans, let them flavor and transfer to a bowl. Place the parsnips in a blender and blend until creamy, combine with the black beans and leeks and serve hot.

Per serving: calories: 219 / fat: 7 / protein: 8 / carbs: 36 /

Nugget Of Zucchini

Prep Time: 15 min
Cook Time: 35 min
Servings: 6

- 200 grams of zucchini
- 1 teaspoon of curry
- 150 grams of natural tofu
- 1 teaspoon of nutritional yeast
- 1 teaspoon of chia seeds
- 3 slices of quinoa bread (see recipe)
- 5 tablespoons of chickpea flour
- 1 pinch of salt
- 1 pinch of black pepper
- 2 tablespoons of olive oil

Wash the courgettes, cut them into julienne strips and cook them for 15 minutes in a non-stick pan with the olive oil. Add the crumbled tofu and cook for another minute. Put the Chia seeds in a bowl with three tablespoons of cold water and leave to rest for 10 minutes. Put the quinoa bread in the blender and grate it. In a bowl, mix the courgettes with the curry, nutritional yeast, salt, pepper, chia seeds and two tablespoons of chickpea flour. In another bowl, mix the remaining chickpea flour with a few tablespoons of water, until you get a thick batter. Make balls with the zucchini-based dough, pass them quickly in the batter and immediately after in the grated quinoa bread. Place the balls on a baking sheet lined with parchment paper and bake at 350° F for about 20-25 minutes. Serve hot.

Per serving: calories: 91 / fat: 6 / protein: 4 / carbs: 5 /

Pumpkin With Miso And Nuts

Prep Time: 10 min
Cook Time: 40 min
Servings: 5

- 1 small pumpkin
- 100 grams of walnuts
- 1/2 cup unsweetened soy yogurt
- 2 tablespoons of miso
- 2 tablespoons of sesame oil
- 1 tablespoon of oregano
- 1 pinch of salt
- 1 pinch of cayenne pepper

Wash the pumpkin well, remove the internal seeds and cut it into wedges of equal size. Line a baking sheet with parchment paper, distribute the slices and grease them with sesame oil and a pinch of salt. Heat the oven to 350° F and bake in a hot oven for about 20-25 minutes. In a bowl, mix well the yogurt, a pinch of pepper and the miso. Finely chop the walnuts. Remove the pumpkin from the oven, spread a little yogurt sauce, oregano and walnuts on each slice. Bake again for about 10 minutes. Serve hot.

Per serving: calories: 173 / fat: 14 / protein: 6 / carbs: 10 /

| Vegan

Zucchini Filled With Hummus And Spinach

Prep Time: 10 min
Cook Time: 45 min
Servings: 6

- 6 large courgettes
- 1 cup of boiled chickpeas
- 1 cup of spinach
- 1 tablespoon of tahini
- the juice of one lemon
- 1 pinch of salt
- 1 pinch of black pepper
- 1 teaspoon of paprika
- 1/2 cup unsweetened coconut yogurt
- 1 tablespoon of olive oil
- 10 chopped almonds
- 1 tablespoon of cilantro

Wash the courgettes, cut them lengthwise into two parts and hollow out the inside with the help of a teaspoon. Line a baking sheet with parchment paper and place the courgettes, bake at 350° F for about 35 minutes. Meanwhile, in a non-stick pan with a tablespoon of olive oil, cook the spinach for about 10-15 minutes, add the salt and pepper. In a bowl, mash the chickpeas with a fork, add the paprika, tahini, lemon juice and spinach and mix well. In a cup, mix the yogurt with the coriander. Chop the almonds. Remove the courgettes from the oven, fill with the chickpea and spinach based sauce, decorate with the yogurt sauce and add the chopped almonds.

Per serving: calories: 96 / fat: 6 / protein: 4 / carbs: 9 /

Millet Meatballs With Broccoli

Prep Time: 10 min
Cook Time: 25 min
Servings: 5

- 2 cups of boiled broccoli
- 200 grams of millet
- 1 yellow potato
- 4 tablespoons of grated quinoa bread (see recipe)
- 2 tablespoons of olive oil
- 1 pinch of salt
- 1 pinch of pepper
- sunflower oil for frying

Peel and boil the potato, drain it and add it to the broccoli. In a bowl, mash the potato and broccoli with a fork, add salt and pepper and a tablespoon of olive oil. Coarsely chop the slices of quinoa bread in a blender. Heat the frying oil in a pan; in the meantime form balls with your hands with the broccoli and potato mixture and pass them in the breadcrumbs. Dip the meatballs in the oil and fry until golden. Remove excess oil by placing the meatballs on paper towels. Serve hot.

Per serving: calories: 245 / fat: 6 / protein: 8 / carbs: 27/

Couscous With Mixed Vegetables

Prep Time: 10 min
Cook Time: 25 min
Servings: 5

- 2 cups of couscous
- 1 cup low sodium vegetable broth
- 2 carrots
- 2 courgettes
- 100 grams of peas
- 100 grams of boiled chickpeas
- 100 grams of boiled black beans
- 10 dried cherry tomatoes
- 1 red pepper
- 1 red onion
- 1 cucumber
- 1 tablespoon of capers
- 4 tablespoons of olive oil
- 1 pinch of salt
- 1 pinch of cayenne pepper
- 1 teaspoon of dried red pepper

Put the couscous in a bowl and mix with a tablespoon of olive oil. Add 2 cups of boiling water and cover. In a non-stick pan heat the remaining olive oil and brown the chopped onion for 5 minutes. Add the broth, julienned zucchini, peas and pepper and cook for about 20 minutes. With a fork, shell the couscous and add the cooked vegetables, chickpeas, beans, chili, capers, diced cucumber, chopped dried tomatoes, and julienned carrots. Serve hot or cold.

Per serving: calories: 266 / fat: 9 / protein: 6 / carbs: 23 /

Farro With Grilled Vegetables

Prep Time: 15 min
Cook Time: 25 min
Servings: 6

- 2 cups of spelled
- 3 zucchini
- 1 eggplant
- 1 red pepper
- 1 yellow pepper
- 2 tomatoes
- 2 tablespoons of chopped fresh mint
- 4 tablespoons of olive oil
- 1 pinch of salt
- 1 pinch of black pepper

Bring plenty of lightly salted water to a boil and cook the farro for about 20-25 minutes, drain well. Clean and cut all the vegetables into slices and put them on a tray. In a glass, prepare an emulsion with olive oil, salt, pepper and mint. Heat the grill. With a pastry brush, grease each slice of vegetables before grilling. Brown the vegetables without burning them. Once all the vegetables are cooked, cut the slices and small strips and mix with the spelled.

Per serving: calories: 343 / fat: 9 / protein: 11 / carbs: 59 /

| Vegan

Buckwheat With Pistachios And Raisins

Prep Time: 15 min
Cook Time: 30 min
Servings: 4

- 200 grams of buckwheat
- 50 grams of raisins
- 2 shallots
- 2 carrots
- 1 boiled turnip
- 1/2 cup of boiled lentils
- 40 grams of pistachios
- 1 tablespoon of Italian seasoning
- 1 tablespoon of minced ginger root
- 5 tablespoons of olive oil
- 1 pinch of salt
- 1 pinch of cayenne pepper

Bring plenty of lightly salted water to a boil and cook the buckwheat for about 15 minutes, drain. Soak the raisins in a bowl of water. In a non-stick pan with two tablespoons of olive oil, brown the thinly sliced shallot for 5 minutes. Add the julienned carrots, diced turnip, lentils and sauté until crisp. Add the chopped pistachios and raisins. In another pan with the remaining oil, put the Italian seasoning, the ginger and sauté the buckwheat. Mix the two preparations and serve.

Per serving: calories: 342 / fat: 19 / protein: 12 / carbs: 55

Pistachio And Pecan Walnuts Granola For Breakfast

Prep Time: 10 min
Cook Time: 10 min
Servings: 13

- 500 grams of oat flakes
- 200 grams of dried figs
- 1/2 cup of coconut water
- 200 grams of cashews
- 200 grams of pecans with pellicle
- 1 pinch of salt
- 1 teaspoon ground cinnamon
- 1 teaspoon of raw cocoa powder

Blend the dried figs with the coconut water in the food processor. Coarsely chop the pecans and cashew nuts. In a bowl, mix well the cashews, pecans, date paste, cinnamon, salt and cocoa. Heat the oven to 350° F. Line a baking sheet with parchment paper. Pour the granola onto the pan, bake for 5 minutes, mix and bake another 5 minutes. This preparation is excellent in the morning with yogurt or to enrich ice cream and puddings.

Per serving: calories: 259 / fat: 19 / protein: 5 / carbs: 22 /

Avocado Stuffed With Spicy Chickpeas And Tofu

Prep Time: 10 min
Cook Time: 0 min
Servings: 4

- 200 grams of boiled chickpeas
- 1 lime
- 3 tomatoes
- 1 white onion
- 1 chili
- 90 grams of tofu
- 2 avocados
- 1 tablespoon of olive oil
- 1 pinch of salt
- 1 pinch of black pepper
- 1 tablespoon of fresh basil

Coarsely crumble the tofu. Chop the chili and onion. Dice the tomatoes. In a bowl put the chickpeas, the lime juice and add the rest of the ingredients except the avocados and mix. Peel the avocados, divide them in half and remove the stone. Stuff the 4 parts of avocado and serve.

Per serving: calories: 376 / fat: 20 / protein: 14 / carbs: 44 /

Seitan Stew With Olives

Prep Time: 5 min
Cook Time: 20 min
Servings: 6

- 500 grams of seitan
- 1 carrot
- 1 red onion
- 2 stalks of celery
- 2 cloves of garlic
- 1 cup of tomato puree
- 1 tablespoon of goji berries
- 2 tablespoons of Italian seasoning
- 1 pinch of salt
- 1 pinch of cayenne pepper
- 1 teaspoon of curry
- 2 tablespoons of olive oil
- 10 black olives

Chop the carrot, the garlic with the celery stalks and the onion and brown in a non-stick pan with the olive oil. Add the chopped seitan, salt, pepper, cook for 5 minutes, stirring and then add the tomato sauce, a couple of tablespoons of boiling water, the Italian seasoning, curry, berries and cook for about 10 more minutes. Add the black olives and serve hot.

Per serving: calories: 239 / fat: 6 / protein: 17 / carbs: 9 /

| Vegan

Piadine Of Chickpeas With Spinach And Mayonnaise

Prep Time: 20 min
Cook Time: 25 min
Servings: 8

- 1/2 cup of coconut milk
- 3/4 cup sunflower oil
- 1 tablespoon of mustard
- the juice of half a lemon
- 1 teaspoon of vinegar
- 1 cup of spinach
- 250 grams of chickpea flour
- 1 pinch of salt
- 1 pinch of black pepper
- 4 tablespoons of olive oil

Put the sunflower oil in a mixer with the coconut milk, the mustard and the vinegar and the lemon and blend at maximum speed for 1 minute; add the vinegar and blend for a minute more. Put the prepared mayonnaise in the refrigerator. Put the chickpea flour in a bowl and slowly mix in the water until the dough is smooth and thick, add a tablespoon of olive oil and a pinch of salt and mix. Put in the refrigerator to rest. Meanwhile, sauté the spinach in a non-stick pan with a pinch of salt and a tablespoon of olive oil. Put the spinach in a bowl, in the same pan, after having greased it with the remaining oil with a kitchen brush, cook the wraps by spoonfuls. Pour a ladle of batter, wait for it to distribute in the pan and dry and turn it to the other side. Continue until the batter is finished. Fill the chickpeas wraps with spinach and mayonnaise.

Per serving: calories: 269 / fat: 14 / protein: 10 / carbs: 23 /

Crunchy Balls Of Garlic Potatoes

Prep Time: 15 min
Cook Time: 10 min
Servings: 2

- 2 large potatoes
- 10 pitted black olives
- 4 cloves of garlic
- 1 pinch of salt
- 1 pinch of black pepper
- 1 tablespoon of thyme
- 5 tablespoons of corn flour

Boil the potatoes in their skins after washing them well. Drain them, let them cool and remove the peel. Finely chop the garlic, olives and thyme. Mash the potatoes with a fork and mix the pulp with the chopped olives, thyme and garlic, add the salt and pepper. Shape into balls and flour them with corn flour. Transfer the balls to a baking sheet covered with parchment paper and bake at 350° F until golden.

Per serving: calories: 195 / fat: 7 / protein: 3 / carbs: 22 /

Cream Of Lentils And Sweet Potatoes

Prep Time: 20 min
Cook Time: 25 min
Servings: 2

- 1 shallot
- 1 teaspoon of curry
- 1 sweet potato
- 150 grams of boiled lentils
- 1 teaspoon of dried thyme
- 2 cups low sodium vegetable broth
- 1 pack of Arabic bread
- 1 carrot
- 1 cucumber
- 1 tomato
- 1 tablespoon of olive oil
- 1 pinch of black pepper
- 1 pinch of salt

In a non-stick pan heat the olive oil and add the chopped shallot, curry, diced sweet potato, salt, thyme and pepper, cook for 5 minutes then add the vegetable broth and cook until the vegetables become soft. Cut the cucumber into strips, the tomato into slices and the carrot into julienne strips. In a food processor, blend the cooked vegetables until you have a sauce. Stuff the Arabian bread with the sauce and raw vegetables.

Per serving: calories: 351 / fat: 9 / protein: 14 / carbs: 57 /

Caramelized Turnips With Hazelnuts

Prep Time: 15 min
Cook Time: 20 min
Servings: 3

- 2 cups of boiled turnips
- 7 tablespoons of fig jam
- 2 tablespoons of red wine vinegar
- 40 black grapes
- 50 grams of hazelnuts
- 1 cup unsweetened soy yogurt
- 2 tablespoons of fresh basil
- 1 pinch of cayenne pepper
- 1 pinch of salt

In a saucepan, mix the fig jam with balsamic vinegar over very low heat. When it has melted, add the boiled turnips and allow them to flavor, add the grapes and cook for another 10 minutes. Add the hazelnuts, salt, pepper, basil and yogurt. Serve hot.

Per serving: calories: 278 / fat: 10 / protein: 4 / carbs: 43 /

| Vegan

Green Beans With Coconut And Almonds

Prep Time: 5 min
Cook Time: 10 min
Servings: 3

- 3 cups of boiled green beans
- 2 tablespoons of coconut butter
- 30 grams of chopped almonds
- 1 pinch of salt
- 1 pinch of pepper
- 2 tablespoons of coconut flakes

In a non-stick pan, melt the coconut butter and brown the green beans for 5 minutes, add the salt and pepper, mix and add the coconut flakes. Cook for another minute and serve hot.

Per serving: calories: 210 / fat: 16 / protein: 5 / carbs: 1

Banana Muffin

Prep Time: 5 min
Cook Time: 20 min
Servings: 8

- 2 bananas
- 150 grams of wholemeal flour
- 2 tablespoons of applesauce
- 1 tablespoon of ground chia seeds
- 2 tablespoons of maple syrup
- 2 cups of coconut milk
- 2 tablespoons of coconut butter
- half a sachet of organic baking powder
- 1 pinch of salt

Soak the ground chia seeds with 3 tablespoons of water. In a bowl put the apple sauce, the soaked chia seeds, the salt, the milk and the butter, mix well. Combine the sifted flour and baking powder, mix again. Blend the bananas in a mixer and incorporate them into the mixture. Fill the muffin tins to three quarters of their capacity and bake in a hot oven at 350° F for about 15-20 minutes.

Per serving: calories: 116 / fat: 4 / protein: 2 / carbs: 18 /

Spelled Pasta With Grapes And Lemon

Prep Time: 5 min
Cook Time: 25 min
Servings: 5

- 400 grams of spelled pasta
- 50 black grapes
- 1 tablespoon of chopped fresh mint
- 1 clove of garlic
- 2 organic lemons
- 1 pinch of salt
- 1 pinch of cayenne pepper
- 3 tablespoons of olive oil

Wash the grapes, and divide them in half. In a non-stick pan heat the oil and brown the minced garlic with the mint, add the grapes and let it flavor, then add the salt and pepper. Remove from the heat and add the grated zest of the lemons. Mix. Cook the pasta in abundant lightly salted boiling water for the cooking time indicated on the package, drain and season with the prepared sauce. Serve hot.

Per serving: calories: 364 / fat: 10 / protein: 11 / carbs: 57 /

Turmeric Sandwiches

Prep Time: 20 min
Cook Time: 25 min
Servings: 10

- 500 grams of celeriac
- 3/4 cup unsweetened rice milk
- 250 grams of wholemeal flour
- 250 grams of rice flour
- 4 tablespoons of olive oil
- 1 sachet of organic dry yeast
- 1 tablespoon of turmeric
- 1 tablespoon of your favorite herbs (basil, mint, thyme, coriander etc.)
- 1 pinch of salt
- 1 pinch of black pepper

Wash the celeriac and cut it into cubes. Cook it in plenty of lightly salted water until it becomes soft, drain well. In a bowl, mix the rice milk with the turmeric and olive oil. In another bowl, mix the flours with the salt, pepper, dry yeast and add the boiled and mashed celeriac with a fork, mix well and add the liquids. Knead with your hands until you get a smooth and homogeneous dough. Heat the oven to 400° F. Prepare muffin molds, pour a generous spoonful of dough into each mold. Cook for about 15-20 minutes.

Per serving: calories: 201 / fat: 6 / protein: 4 / carbs: 32 /

| Vegan

Fish & Seafood

Wholemeal Rice With Cod And Pine Nuts

Prep Time: 10 min **Cook Time:** 30 min **Servings:** 4

- 2 cups of brown rice
- 4 tablespoons of pine nuts
- 6 courgettes
- 2 cloves of garlic
- 1 organic lemon
- 4 tablespoons of olive oil
- 200 grams of boiled cod
- 1 pinch of salt
- 1 pinch of black pepper
- 10 cherry tomatoes

Cook the rice in plenty of lightly salted water for about 15-20 minutes. In a non-stick pan, lightly toast the pine nuts. Wash the courgettes and cut them into cubes, wash the cherry tomatoes and cut them into four parts. Peel the garlic and cut into very thin slices, wash the lemon and grate the zest. In a non-stick pan heat the olive oil and brown the garlic for 1 minute, add the diced cod and continue cooking, stirring for 5 minutes. Add the cherry tomatoes, courgettes, lemon zest and cook for another 10 minutes. Add salt and pepper. Drain the rice well and add it to the other ingredients. Season with the toasted pine nuts.

Per serving: calories: 327 / fat: 15 / protein: 17 / carbs: 28 /

Salmon With Rocket Pesto

Prep Time: 10 min **Cook Time:** 10 min **Servings:** 4

- 4 wild salmon fillets
- 2 tablespoons of parsley
- 1 cup of rocket
- 2 cloves of garlic
- 1 organic lemon
- 3 tablespoons of olive oil
- 5 tablespoons of cashews
- 1 pinch of salt
- 1 pinch of cayenne pepper

Wash and put the rocket, garlic, cashews, a pinch of salt and a tablespoon of oil in a mixer and blend well. Put the pesto obtained in the refrigerator. Wash the salmon, brush it with oil and place it on a baking sheet covered with parchment paper at 400° F for about 10 minutes.
Remove the salmon from the oven and cover it with the pesto.

Per serving: calories: 346 / fat: 27 / protein: 18 / carbs: 7 /

Tuna Croutons

Prep Time: 10 min
Cook Time: 0 min
Servings: 6

- 200 grams of tuna in water
- 2 tablespoons of unsweetened soy yogurt
- 2 teaspoons of olive oil
- 1 tablespoon of thyme
- 1 teaspoon of turmeric
- 1 pinch of salt
- 1 pinch of pepper
- 6 corn cakes

Drain the water from the tuna very well. Put the tuna, soy yogurt, salt, pepper, thyme and olive oil in a blender. Blend for 1 minute and stuff the biscuits.

Per serving: calories: 97 / fat: 5 / protein: 7 / carbs: 6 /

Cabbage With Anchovies

Prep Time: 10 min
Cook Time: 0 min
Servings: 2

- 2 cups of boiled cabbage
- 2 tablespoons of capers
- 5 anchovies in oil
- 2 tomatoes
- 1 chili
- 2 tablespoons of olive oil
- 1 pinch of salt
- 1 pinch of cayenne pepper
- 1 tablespoon of chopped fresh parsley

In a bowl, mix well the anchovies cut into small pieces, the chopped chili pepper, the parsley, the whole capers, the diced tomatoes, the oil, the salt, the pepper. Add the cabbage and mix again.

Per serving: calories: 257 / fat: 19 / protein: 12 / carbs: 11 /

| Fish & Seafood

Wholemeal Pasta With Sardines And Leeks

Prep Time: 5 min | **Cook Time:** 15 min | **Servings:** 3

- 200 grams of wholemeal pasta
- 2 leeks
- 1 basket of radicchio
- 8 clean sardines
- 2 tablespoons of olive oil
- 1 pinch of salt
- 1 pinch of pepper

Clean and cut the leeks into thin slices. In a non-stick pan sauté the leeks with the oil, the chopped radicchio and the sardines cut into small pieces, add the salt and pepper and cook, stirring for 10 minutes. In a pot with plenty of lightly salted boiling water, cook the pasta for the cooking time indicated on the package, drain well and season with the prepared sardine sauce.

Per serving: calories: 237 / fat: 11 / protein: 13 / carbs: 22

Salmon Salad With Mushrooms And Broccoli

Prep Time: 5 min | **Cook Time:** 10 min | **Servings:** 2

- 200 grams of smoked wild salmon
- 100 grams of cremini mushrooms
- 1 cup of boiled broccoli
- 2 tablespoons of chopped parsley
- 2 tablespoons of olive oil
- 1 pinch of salt
- 1 pinch of cayenne pepper
- 1 organic lemon

Cut the salmon into strips and marinate in the lemon juice. Wash the mushrooms, cut them into very thin slices and add them to the salmon. In a non-stick pan heat the oil and pour the broccoli, add the salt and pepper and brown for 5 minutes. Drain the lemon juice from the salmon and mushrooms and put them in a bowl, add the broccoli and parsley and serve.

Per serving: calories: 298 / fat: 19 / protein: 26 / carbs: 4 /

Anti inflammatory Diet Cookbook for Beginners 2022

Hake With Caper Sauce And Dried Tomatoes

Prep Time 5 min **Cook Time** 10 min **Servings** 4

- 400 grams of hake fillets
- 2 tablespoons of capers
- 10 dried cherry tomatoes
- 3/4 cup unsweetened coconut yogurt
- 2 tablespoons of olive oil
- 1 pinch of salt
- 1 pinch of black pepper
- 1 teaspoon of turmeric
- 1 tablespoon of cilantro

Heat the olive oil in a non-stick pan, add the hake fillets and cook for about 5 minutes per side, add the salt and pepper. Put the coconut yogurt with the coriander, turmeric, dried tomatoes and capers in a blender and blend for one minute at high speed. Serve the fillets with the sauce.

Per serving: calories: 209 / fat: 12 / protein: 19 / carbs: 6 /

Sole Filets With Fennel In Paperboard

Prep Time 15 min **Cook Time** 25 min **Servings** 3

- 700 grams of sole fillets
- 2 cloves of garlic
- 1 tablespoon of chopped parsley
- 1 chili
- 3 fennel
- 4 tablespoons of olive oil
- 1 pinch of salt
- 1 pinch of pepper
- 1 lemon

Chop the garlic and add it to the parsley and put it in a bowl with the chili, salt, pepper and lemon juice; mix well. Wash the sole fillets and marinate them in the preparation for 15 minutes. Meanwhile, cut squares of baking paper. After 15 minutes, place each fillet on a piece of paper, without draining the marinade and add a few slices of fennel. Close the paper and place on a baking sheet. Heat the oven to 350° F and bake the packets for about 25 minutes.

Per serving: calories: 337 / fat: 16 / protein: 39 / carbs: 7 /

| Fish & Seafood

Brown Rice With Tuna, Peppers And Rocket

Prep Time: 10 min
Cook Time: 25 min
Servings: 4

- 200 grams of brown rice
- 200 grams of tuna in water
- 1 red pepper
- 1 yellow pepper
- 1 shallot
- 1 cup of rocket
- 2 tablespoons of olive oil
- 1 pinch of salt
- 1 pinch of black pepper

Clean the peppers, remove the stalk, cut it in half and remove the seeds. Cut them into strips. Chop the shallot. In a non-stick pan heat the oil and brown the chopped shallot for 3 minutes. Add the peppers and cook, add salt and pepper and cook until they become soft. In a pot of lightly salted boiling water, cook the rice for about 15 minutes, drain it flat and mix it with the peppers, the tuna drained from the water and the chopped rocket.

Per serving: calories: 226 / fat: 8 / protein: 17 / carbs: 25 /

Cod And Pumpkin Fishballs With White Sauce

Prep Time: 10 min
Cook Time: 25 min
Servings: 4

- 200 grams of cod
- 1 cup boiled pumpkin cubes
- 1 cup unsweetened soy yogurt
- 1 tablespoon of mustard
- 5 tablespoons of grated wholemeal bread
- 3 tablespoons of corn flour
- 5 tablespoons of olive oil
- 1 tablespoon of chopped parsley
- 1 pinch of salt
- 1 pinch of pepper

Put the yogurt, mustard and parsley in the mixer and chop. Set the sauce aside. In a non-stick pan with a tablespoon of oil, cook the cod for 5 minutes and then chop it coarsely. Mash the pumpkin with a fork, add the cod and a tablespoon of oil, a pinch of salt and a pinch of pepper, and a tablespoon of breadcrumbs. Mix the ingredients well and shape into balls with your hands. Dip the balls in the cornmeal mixed with the breadcrumbs and place them on a baking sheet lined with parchment paper. Heat the oven to 400° F and bake for 10 minutes. Serve with the sauce.

Per serving: calories: 233 / fat: 13 / protein: 16 / carbs: 3 /

Mackerel With Sesame And Soy Sprouts

Prep Time: 15 min
Cook Time: 10 min
Servings: 5

- 400 grams of mackerel fillets in oil
- 2 yellow peppers
- 2 cloves of garlic
- 200 grams of red beans
- 1 tablespoon of capers
- 1 cup of bean sprouts
- 1 organic lemon
- 1 tablespoon of sesame seeds
- 2 tablespoons of olive oil
- 1 pinch of salt
- 1 pinch of black pepper

Chop the garlic. In a non-stick pan heat a tablespoon of olive oil. Clean the peppers by removing the stalk, cutting them in two and removing the seeds inside. Cut the peppers into strips. Sauté the garlic in the oil for a minute, then add the peppers, capers and pepper and cook until soft. Crumble the mackerel fillets with your hands after draining them from the excess oil and mix with the sesame seeds. In a bowl combine the mackerel, peppers, bean sprouts and mix well.

Per serving: calories: 346 / fat: 22 / protein: 20 / carbs: 17 /

Quinoa With Tuna Pesto

Prep Time: 10 min
Cook Time: 20 min
Servings: 4

- 400 grams of quinoa
- 200 grams of tuna in water
- 100 grams of feta
- 1 tomato
- 1 cucumber
- 1 tablespoon of hazelnuts
- 1 tablespoon of chopped basil
- 1 pinch of salt
- 1 pinch of cayenne pepper
- 1 tablespoon of olive oil

Cook the quinoa in plenty of lightly salted boiling water for 15-20 minutes and drain well. Put the tuna in the blender with the feta, hazelnuts, basil and olive oil and blend until smooth. Wash and dice the tomato. Remove the peel from the cucumber and cut it into thin slices. Combine the quinoa with the vegetables and the sauce and mix well.

Per serving: calories: 262 / fat: 9 / protein: 22 / carbs: 25 /

| Fish & Seafood

Soup Of Oysters And Mushrooms

Prep Time: 10 min
Cook Time: 50 min
Servings: 6

- 15 oysters
- 1 teaspoon of oregano
- 1 teaspoon of thyme
- 1 cup of white mushrooms
- 2 cups low sodium vegetable broth
- 1 onion
- 1 leek
- 1 yellow potato
- 1 tablespoon of coconut butter

In a non-stick pan, melt the coconut butter and brown the chopped onion and leek. Add the sliced mushrooms, mix and after a minute add the vegetable broth and cook for 20 minutes over moderate heat. Add the thyme and oregano. Cut the potato into cubes, add it and cook for another 20 minutes. Wash the oysters well, put them in a saucepan with the lid on low heat to make them open. Once opened, extract the molluscs and filter the liquid they have released with a strainer. Add the liquid to the mushrooms and potatoes. Cook for another 3 minutes, add the oysters, mix and serve.

Per serving: calories: 101 / fat: 8 / protein: 7 / carbs: 9 /

Millet With Asparagus, Almonds And Sardines

Prep Time: 5 min
Cook Time: 20 min
Servings: 6

- 400 grams of millet
- 300 grams of asparagus
- 300 grams of sardines in oil
- 1 orange
- 1 clove of garlic
- 30 grams of almonds
- 1 pinch of salt
- 1 pinch of cayenne pepper
- 6 fresh mint leaves

Wash and chop the asparagus. In a pot of lightly salted boiling water, cook the millet for 5 minutes, add the asparagus and continue to cook for 10 more minutes, drain well. Crumble the sardines with your hands. Chop the garlic with the almonds and fresh mint leaves. Squeeze the orange. Combine the millet with the sardines, the orange juice and the chopped herbs and serve.

Per serving: calories: 273 / fat: 14 / protein: 19 / carbs: 16 /

Rolls Of Aubergines With Cod With Mediterranean Aromas

Prep Time 30 min | **Cook Time** 10 min | **Servings** 10

- 20 slices of grilled eggplant
- 200 grams of cod fillet
- 15 dried cherry tomatoes
- 20 lettuce leaves
- 1 cup unsweetened soy yogurt
- 1 teaspoon of dried sage
- 1 teaspoon of dried basil
- 1 teaspoon of dried parsley
- 1 pinch of salt
- 1 pinch of cayenne pepper
- 3 tablespoons of olive oil
- 1 red onion
- 2 cloves of garlic

Put the soy yogurt with the onion, the herbs, 1 tablespoon of olive oil in the mixer and blend well. Coarsely chop the cherry tomatoes with garlic. In a non-stick pan, heat the olive oil and cook the cod fillets for 5 minutes on each side, add the salt and pepper. Let them cool and then chop them coarsely. Take a slice of aubergine and spread it with the yogurt sauce, add a salad leaf, add the chopped cod, the cherry tomatoes and close the roll with a toothpick. Repeat for all eggplant slices and serve.

Per serving: calories: 78 / fat: 4 / protein: 5 / carbs: 5 /

Tomatoes Stuffed With Tuna And Chickpeas

Prep Time 20 min | **Cook Time** 0 min | **Servings** 4

- 4 large tomatoes
- 1 cup of boiled chickpeas
- 500 grams of tuna in water
- 8 tablespoons of ricotta cheese
- 2 tablespoons of chopped fresh basil
- 2 tablespoons of olive oil
- 1 pinch of salt
- 1 pinch of pepper

Wash the tomatoes and cut them into two parts. With the help of a teaspoon empty the inside. In a bowl, combine the chickpeas boiled with basil, ricotta, olive oil, salt, pepper and the tuna drained from excess water. Mix well and stuff the tomatoes with the mixture.

Per serving: calories: 293 / fat: 14 / protein: 28 / carbs: 18 /

| Fish & Seafood

Seaweed Fritters Nori And Carrots

Prep Time: 5 min
Cook Time: 20 min
Servings: 6

- 3 carrots
- 1 white onion
- 7 tablespoons of rice flour
- 2 tablespoons of sesame oil
- 2 sheets of nori seaweed
- 1 pinch of salt
- sunflower oil for frying

Grate the carrots and onion; cut the nori seaweed into very small squares. Mix the rice flour with the salt, add water until you get a very thick paste, add the vegetables and mix well. In a pan heat the sunflower oil; when it is very hot pour the mixture in spoonfuls and cook the pancakes until they are golden on both sides. Season with a pinch of salt and serve hot.

Per serving: calories: 148 / fat: 4 / protein: 2 / carbs: 23 /

Cod With Creamy Onions

Prep Time: 5 min
Cook Time: 35 min
Servings: 4

- 500 grams of mackerel in oil
- 1 organic lemon
- 2 cloves of garlic
- 4 tablespoons of olive oil
- 6 white onions
- 4 tablespoons of maple syrup
- 2 oranges
- 1 salt lace
- 1 pinch of pepper

Chop the onions and put them in a non-stick saucepan with 1 tablespoon of olive oil; brown for 5 minutes. Set the heat to low, add 6 tablespoons of water, the orange juice and maple syrup, cook covered for about 20 minutes, check that the boil is at minimum and that the onions do not burn. Drain the mackerel from the oil, and put it to marinate in the remaining oil mixed with the minced garlic, a pinch of salt, a pinch of pepper and the lemon juice.
Serve the mackerel with the creamy onions.

Per serving: calories: 559 / fat: 32 / protein: 31 / carbs: 38 /

Anti inflammatory Diet Cookbook for Beginners 2022

Squid Rings With Saffron

Prep Time 10 min **Cook Time** 15 min **Servings** 4

- 500 grams of squid rings
- 2 tomatoes
- 1/4 cup low sodium vegetable broth
- 1 red onion
- 1 tablespoon of thyme
- 1 sachet of saffron
- 4 tablespoons of olive oil
- 1 salt lace
- 1 pinch of cayenne pepper

Wash and cut the tomatoes into cubes. Chop the onion and brown it for 5 minutes in a non-stick pan with a tablespoon of olive oil. Add the squid rings, cook for a minute, add the salt and pepper and then add the broth and cook for another two minutes. In another pan heat the remaining oil and brown the thyme with the saffron and diced tomatoes, add a pinch of salt and cayenne pepper and cook for about 5 minutes. Pour the tomatoes over the squid and serve hot.

Per serving: calories: 266 / fat: 16 / protein: 22 / carbs: 38 /

Cod In Grapefruit Cups

Prep Time 5 min **Cook Time** 15 min **Servings** 3

- 3 grapefruits
- 300 grams of cod fillets
- 2 tablespoons of olive oil
- 1 tablespoon of parsley
- 6 salad leaves of your choice
- 1 tomato
- 1 tablespoon of balsamic vinegar
- 1 pinch of salt
- 1 pinch of black pepper
- 1 lemon

Wash the grapefruits and cut them in half; with the help of a teaspoon empty the internal pulp. In a non-stick pan, heat the oil and cook the cod fillets for 5 minutes on each side, add the salt, lemon juice and pepper. Break the salad leaves into small pieces with your hands. Wash and dice the tomato. In a bowl combine the tomato, salad, lacceto and cod cut into pieces and mix well. Stuff the grapefruits with the fish and serve.

Per serving: calories: 260 / fat: 10 / protein: 19 / carbs: 22 /

| Fish & Seafood

Clams With Chickpeas

Prep Time: 10 min
Cook Time: 20 min
Servings: 7

- 800 grams of clams
- 2 cups of boiled chickpeas
- 2 cloves of garlic
- 4 tablespoons of olive oil
- 1 tablespoon of balsamic vinegar
- 1 red onion
- 1 tablespoon of basil
- 1 pinch of salt
- 1 pinch of pepper

Put the clams in a bowl of cold water for two hours, then wash them well. Heat a thick-bottomed pan and pour the clams with the garlic cloves, chopped onion and basil. Season with oil and cook over a covered heat until the clams open. Shell the clams and put them in a bowl with the chickpeas, mix well and serve. Season with the balsamic vinegar, salt and pepper.

Per serving: calories: 349 / fat: 12 / protein: 35 / carbs: 26 /

Sauce For Croutons With Salmon

Prep Time: 5 min
Cook Time: 0 min
Servings: 6

- 300 grams of smoked salmon
- 1 cup unsweetened soy yogurt
- 300 grams of boiled shrimp
- 2 tablespoons of lemon juice
- 1 teaspoon of turmeric
- 1 pinch of salt
- 1 pinch of black pepper

Put all the ingredients in a blender and blend on high speed for one minute. This sauce is perfect for filling croutons, enriching crepes with grilled vegetables or for dressing pasta.

Per serving: calories: 116 / fat: 5 / protein: 15 / carbs: 1 /

Snacks

Sticks With Sesame And Turmeric

Prep Time: 5 min **Cook Time:** 10 min **Servings:** 10

- 140 grams of almond flour
- 40 grams of sesame seeds
- 2 egg whites
- 1 pinch of salt
- 1 pinch of pepper
- 1 teaspoon of turmeric

Mix the flour with the salt, pepper and turmeric. Add the sesame seeds and mix again. Beat the egg whites and mix well. Line a baking sheet with parchment paper, divide the dough into 10 and form cylinders with your hands. Cook at 350° F for about 10 minutes.

Per serving: calories: 91 / fat: 7 / protein: 4 / carbs: 3 /

Quinoa And Lemon Cookies

Prep Time: 20 min **Cook Time:** 25 min **Servings:** 10

- 400 grams of wholemeal flour
- 250 grams of quinoa flour
- 5 tablespoons of ghee
- 1 organic lemon
- 4 tablespoons of maple syrup
- 1 teaspoon of cardamom powder
- 1 pinch of salt

Cook the quinoa in a pot of unsalted boiling water for about 15 minutes, drain well and let it cool. Mix the two flours with the salt and cardamom. Grate the lemon zest and add it to the flour, mix. Combine lemon juice, maple syrup and ghee and knead. If the dough is too dry, add a few tablespoons of vegetable milk of your choice. Roll out the dough and form discs. Line a baking sheet, arrange the discs and bake at 350° F for about 10 minutes.

Per serving: calories: 241 / fat: 5 / protein: 8 / carbs: 42 /

| Snacks

Apple And Cinnamon Chips

Prep Time 20 min | **Cook Time** 120 min | **Servings** 2

- 2 apples
- 1 teaspoon ground cinnamon
- 1 teaspoon of vanilla powder
- 1 teaspoon of ghee
- 2 limes

Squeeze the limes, add the cinnamon, ghee and vanilla powder to the juice and mix well. Peel the apples into very thin slices. Heat the oven to 200° F. With the help of a kitchen brush, grease the apples on both sides and spread them on a baking sheet lined with baking paper. Cook for about two hours, checking often.

Per serving: calories: 158 / fat: 3 / protein: 2 / carbs: 36 /

Celery With Curry Sauce

Prep Time 15 min | **Cook Time** 0 min | **Servings** 3

- 1 celery
- 1 cup unsweetened soy yogurt
- 1 teaspoon of curry
- 1 pinch of salt
- 1 teaspoon of fennel seeds

Wash the celery and cut it into small sticks. Mix the soy yogurt with the curry, the salt, and the crushed fennel seeds with the pestle. Place the celery sticks in a tray with the sauce in the shot glasses.

Per serving: calories: 60 / fat: 1 / protein: 3 / carbs: 8 /

Skewers Of Tofu And Zucchini

Prep Time: 5 min
Cook Time: 5 min
Servings: 6

- 200 grams of smoked tofu
- 2 courgettes
- 2 tablespoons of olive oil
- 1 pinch of salt
- 1 pinch of red pepper

Cut the tofu into cubes and brown it for 5 minutes in a non-stick pan with a tablespoon of oil. Cut the courgettes into slices, and with the help of a kitchen brush, grease them with the oil previously mixed with the salt and chili pepper. Grill the courgettes without letting them burn. Place a cube of tofu alternating with a slice of courgette on a skewer toothpick, repeat. Continue until all ingredients are consumed.

Per serving: calories: 127 / fat: 9 / protein: 8 / carbs: 4 /

Rösti Potatoes With Rosemary

Prep Time: 5 min
Cook Time: 10 min
Servings: 3

- 3 yellow potatoes
- 1 red onion
- 10 cashews
- 1 tablespoon of powdered rosemary
- 1 pinch of salt
- 1 pinch of cayenne pepper
- 2 tablespoons of olive oil

Peel the potatoes and grate them. Place them in a clean cloth and squeeze well to remove excess water. Mix the potatoes with a pinch of salt, pepper, rosemary, chopped cashews and chopped onion. Heat the oil in a non-stick pan and cook the dough in spoonfuls for 5 minutes per side.

Per serving: calories: 287 / fat: 12 / protein: 5 / carbs: 42 /

| Snacks

Sweets With Carrots And Chocolate

Prep Time: 20 min
Cook Time: 25 min
Servings: 4

- 4 tablespoons of maple syrup
- 50 grams of wholemeal flour
- 50 grams of almond flour
- 3 tablespoons of raw cocoa powder
- 1 teaspoon ground cinnamon
- The zest of an organic lemon
- 2 organic eggs
- 3 tablespoons of ghee
- 4 tablespoons of coconut milk
- 100 grams of grated carrots
- 1 teaspoon of baking soda
- 1 teaspoon of cardamom
- 1 pinch of salt

In a bowl, mix the flours with the baking soda, cardamom, cocoa, cinnamon and lemon zest. Beat the eggs with the coconut milk, carrots, salt and maple syrup. Combine the two compounds and mix well. Fill the muffin tins three-quarters full and bake in a hot oven at 350° F for about 25 minutes.

Per serving: calories: 214 / fat: 13 / protein: 8 / carbs: 17 /

Chestnut Panini With Fennels

Prep Time: 15 min
Cook Time: 30 min
Servings: 5

- 100 grams of boiled chestnuts
- 1 tablespoon of goji berries
- 1 tablespoon of olive oil
- 1 shallot
- 100 grams of fennel
- 2 teaspoons of dried sage
- 2 teaspoons of organic lemon zest
- 1/2 cup of orange juice
- 50 grams of grated quinoa bread (see recipe)
- 5 pecans with pellicle
- 1 organic egg
- 1 cup of blueberries

Put the goji berries in a bowl of cold water for 10 minutes, drain well. In a non-stick pan heat the oil and brown the shallot with the chopped fennel for 5 minutes, add a few tablespoons of boiling water and continue cooking until soft. Put the boiled chestnuts in a bowl, add the soaked goji berries, the browned fennel and shallot, the orange juice, the blueberries, the lemon zest, the chopped walnuts and the beaten egg. Grease a loaf pan with oil and pour the dough. Level with the back of a spoon soaked in cold water and sprinkle with grated quinoa bread. Heat the oven to 350° F and bake for about 30 minutes. Cut into slices.

Per serving: calories: 128 / fat: 6 / protein: 3 / carbs: 92 /

Anti inflammatory Diet Cookbook for Beginners 2022

Oat Bars With Cocoa And Honey

Prep Time: 10 min   **Cook Time:** 10 min   **Servings:** 7

- 15 tablespoons of oat flakes
- 12 tablespoons of pecans with pellicle
- 12 tablespoons of raw honey
- 2 tablespoons of raw cocoa

Crumble the pecans and roast them for 2 minutes, stirring constantly, in a non-stick pan. In a bowl, mix the toasted walnuts with the honey, cocoa and oats. Spread the mixture on a baking sheet lined with parchment paper and cover with another sheet of parchment paper. Press lightly with a kitchen rolling pin. Heat the baking tray to 320° F and bake after removing the top sheet. Cook for about 10 minutes. Remove from the oven, allow to cool and cut into bars.

Per serving: calories: 345 / fat: 15 / protein: 10 / carbs: 46 /

Sesame And Paprika Crackers

Prep Time: 5 min   **Cook Time:** 25 min   **Servings:** 9

- 160 grams of quinoa
- 3 tablespoons of sesame seeds
- 1 tablespoon of Italian seasoning
- 1 pinch of paprika
- 1 pinch of salt
- 4 tablespoons of olive oil

Bring a pot of lightly salted boiling water to a boil and cook the quinoa for about 15 minutes, drain well. Put three quarters of the quinoa in the blender and blend with the olive oil, salt and paprika. Transfer the mixture to a bowl and combine with the spices and sesame seeds. Roll out the dough on a baking sheet covered with baking paper and cover with another sheet, roll out with a kitchen rolling pin, without pressing. Gently remove the top sheet and bake in a hot oven at 350° F for about 10 minutes. cut the crackers to the desired size.

Per serving: calories: 124 / fat: 8 / protein: 3 / carbs: 12 /

| Snacks

Turmeric Focaccia With Nuts

Prep Time: 10 min
Cook Time: 15 min
Servings: 6

- 240 grams of spelled flour
- 60 grams of wholemeal flour
- 2 tablespoons of turmeric
- 3 tablespoons of walnuts
- 1 teaspoon of organic dry yeast
- 1 cup of water
- 1 pinch of salt
- 1 tablespoon of olive oil

Combine the spelled flour, turmeric, wholemeal flour, chopped walnuts, salt, dry yeast and mix. Slowly add the water and mix well. Grease a pan with olive oil, pour the mixture and bake at 400° F for about 15 minutes.

Per serving: calories: 177 / fat: 2 / protein: 7 / carbs: 34 /

Pear And Cinnamon Pudding

Prep Time: 10 min
Cook Time: 0 min
Servings: 2

- 2 pears
- 60 grams of low fat cottage cheese
- 1 organic lemon
- 1 tablespoon of maple syrup
- 1 tablespoon of ground cinnamon
- 1 tablespoon of chopped hazelnuts

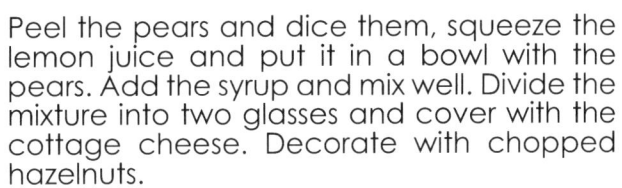

Peel the pears and dice them, squeeze the lemon juice and put it in a bowl with the pears. Add the syrup and mix well. Divide the mixture into two glasses and cover with the cottage cheese. Decorate with chopped hazelnuts.

Per serving: calories: 115 / fat: 0 / protein: 1 / carbs: 31 /

Anti inflammatory Diet Cookbook for Beginners 2022

Peanut Butter Toast With Vegetables

Prep Time: 10 min
Cook Time: 0 min
Servings: 2

- 4 slices of wholemeal toast bread
- 1 tablespoon of peanut butter
- 1 cucumber
- 1 onion
- 1 tomato
- 1 tablespoon of chopped fresh basil

Toast the toast slices without burning them, spread the peanut butter on two slices. Peel the cucumber and cut it into slices, chop the onion, wash and slice the tomato. Put the cucumber slices on top of the buttered bread slices, add the tomato slices, the chopped onion and close the toast with the other slices of bread.

Per serving: calories: 220 / fat: 5 / protein: 8 / carbs: 35 /

Strawberries, Lemon And Mint

Prep Time: 10 min
Cook Time: 5 min
Servings: 3

- 2 cups of strawberries
- 1 tablespoon of maple syrup
- 1 tablespoon of chopped fresh mint leaves
- 2 organic lemons
- 100 grams of 70% dark chocolate

Wash the strawberries and cut them into cubes. Squeeze the lemon juice and mix it with the maple syrup and mint. Add the strawberries and leave them to flavor for a few minutes. Meanwhile, melt the chocolate in a bain-marie, Put the strawberries in three bowls and add the hot dark chocolate.

Per serving: calories: 237 / fat: 15 / protein: 3 / carbs: 24 /

| Snacks

Banana And Hazelnut Cookies

Prep Time: 5 min
Cook Time: 10 min
Servings: 4

- 2 bananas
- 1 tablespoon of chopped toasted hazelnuts
- 60 grams of coconut flour
- 60 grams of wholemeal flour
- 1 pinch of salt
- 1 teaspoon of raw honey
- 2 pitted dates

Mix the wholemeal flour with the coconut flour, the salt and the chopped hazelnuts. Finely chop the dates and mash the bananas with a fork until they are pureed. Mix the dates and honey with the bananas and add to the flour, mixing well. Line a baking sheet with parchment paper and with your hands make balls of dough and crush them lightly, arrange the biscuits in the pan and bake at 350° F for about 10 minutes.

Per serving: calories: 210 / fat: 5 / protein: 5 / carbs: 40 /

Oranges Stuffed With Banana And Blueberries

Prep Time: 10 minutes + 2 hours of rest
Cook Time: 0 min
Servings: 6

- 3 oranges
- 1 cup of blueberries
- 2 bananas
- 2 tablespoons of maple syrup

Peel the bananas and cut them into small pieces. In a bowl, mix the bananas with the blueberries and maple syrup, place in an airtight bag and place in the freezer for 2 hours. Wash the oranges well, divide them in half and with the help of a teaspoon empty the internal pulp. Put the oranges in the freezer as well. After the two hours, put the bananas and blueberries in a mixer and blend well. Stuff the oranges with the pureed fruit.

Per serving: calories: 86 / fat: 0 / protein: 1 / carbs: 22 /

Smoothies & Juices

Spirulina Smoothie And Fresh Fruit

Prep Time 5 min **Cook Time** 0 min **Servings** 2

- 1 banana
- 1 teaspoon of blue spirulina
- 1 teaspoon of peanut butter
- 2 cups of almond milk
- 1 cup of blueberries
- 1 tablespoon of coconut flakes
- 1 tablespoon of granola

Put the peeled banana, spirulina, peanut butter, milk and blueberries with 6 ice cubes in a blender and blend on high speed for 1 minute. Pour into glasses and add the granola and coconut flakes.

Per serving: calories: 180 / fat: 10 / protein: 5 / carbs: 53 /

Acai Smoothie

Prep Time 5 min **Cook Time** 0 min **Servings** 2

- 1 tablespoon of acai berries
- 1 banana
- 1/2 cup of strawberries
- 1/2 cup of blueberries
- 1 teaspoon of cinnamon
- 1 cup of coconut water
- 1 cup of almond milk
- 2 dragon fruit
- a few mint leaves

Put all the ingredients in the blender with 8 ice cubes and blend on high speed for one minute. Garnish with mint leaves and serve.

Per serving: calories: 166 / fat: 2 / protein: 3 / carbs: 36 /

| Smoothies & Juices

Morning Smoothie

Prep Time: 5 min | **Cook Time:** 0 min | **Servings:** 2

- 1 cucumber
- 1 turnip cleaned and diced
- 1 peeled green apple
- 1 teaspoon of cilantro
- 1 teaspoon of minced ginger
- 1 cup of coconut milk

Put all the ingredients in the blender with 8 ice cubes and blend on high speed for one minute.

Per serving: calories: 112 / fat: 5 / protein: 1 / carbs: 17 /

Watermelon & Lemongrass Smoothie

Prep Time: 5 min | **Cook Time:** 0 min | **Servings:** 2

- 1 cup of watermelon
- 1 teaspoon of chopped fresh basil
- 1 teaspoon of grated ginger root
- 1 teaspoon of lemongrass
- 2 cups unsweetened almond milk

Put all the ingredients in the blender with 8 ice cubes and blend on high speed for one minute.

Per serving: calories: 62 / fat: 3 / protein: 3 / carbs: 9 /

Mango & Dragon Fruit Smoothie

Prep Time: 5 min
Cook Time: 0 min
Servings: 2

- 2 dragon fruit
- 1 cup of mango
- 1 cup of coconut water
- 1 cup of coconut milk
- 1 teaspoon of chopped fresh mint leaves
- the juice of an organic lime

Put all the ingredients in the blender with 8 ice cubes and blend on high speed for one minute.

Per serving: calories: 101 / fat: 3 / protein: 1 / carbs: 18

Smoothie Papaya & Pineapple

Prep Time: 5 min
Cook Time: 0 min
Servings: 2

- 2 cups unsweetened coconut milk
- 1 teaspoon of turmeric
- 1 teaspoon of grated ginger
- 1 cup of papaya
- 1 pinch of black pepper
- 2 slices of pineapple

Put all the ingredients in the blender with 8 ice cubes and blend on high speed for one minute.

Per serving: calories: 236 / fat: 10 / protein: 2 / carbs: 36 /

Green Smoothie

Prep Time: 5 min

Cook Time: 0 min

Servings: 2

- 1/2 cup of kale
- 1/2 cup of spinach
- 1 stalk of celery
- 1 cucumber
- 1 banana
- 2 cups unsweetened coconut milk

Put all the ingredients in the blender with 8 ice cubes and blend on high speed for one minute.

Per serving: calories: 109 / fat: 5 / protein: 1 / carbs: 17 /

Almond & Carrots Smoothie

Prep Time: 5 min

Cook Time: 0 min

Servings: 2

- 2 carrots
- 2 stalks of celery
- 1 tablespoon of almonds
- 2 cups of almond milk
- 1 cup of spinach

Put all the ingredients in the blender with 8 ice cubes and blend on high speed for one minute.

Per serving: calories: 82 / fat: 3 / protein: 3 / carbs: 12 /

Anti inflammatory Diet Cookbook for Beginners 2022

Almond & Orange Smoothie

Prep Time: 5 min **Cook Time:** 0 min **Servings:** 2

- 1 tablespoon of pecans
- 1 tablespoon of turmeric
- 2 peeled oranges
- 1 teaspoon of maple syrup
- 2 cups unsweetened almond milk

Put all the ingredients in the blender with 8 ice cubes and blend on high speed for one minute.

Per serving: calories: 145 / fat: 6 / protein: 3 / carbs: 23 /

Beet And Mango Smoothie

Prep Time: 5 min **Cook Time:** 0 min **Servings:** 2

- 1 beetroot
- 10 black grapes
- 1 mango
- the juice of 1 lime
- 2 cups of unsweetened soy milk

Put all the ingredients in the blender with 8 ice cubes and blend on high speed for one minute.

Per serving: calories: 214 / fat: 8 / protein: 9 / carbs: 29 /

| Smoothies & Juices

Beet And Apple Smoothie

Prep Time: 5 min
Cook Time: 0 min
Servings: 2

- 1 cup of chard
- 1 banana
- 2 peeled oranges
- 1 green apple

Put all the ingredients in the blender with 8 ice cubes and blend on high speed for one minute.

Per serving: calories: 216 / fat: 8 / protein: 9 / carbs: 29 /

Strawberries Hazelnuts Smoothie

Prep Time: 5 min
Cook Time: 0 min
Servings: 2

- 1 tablespoon of hazelnuts
- 1 cup of strawberries
- 1 tablespoon of chia seeds
- a few fresh mint leaves
- 2 cups unsweetened coconut milk
- 1 teaspoon of honey

Put all the ingredients in the blender with 8 ice cubes and blend on high speed for one minute.

Per serving: calories: 102 / fat: 7 / protein: 2 / carbs: 8 /

Peaches And Kiwi Smoothie

Prep Time: 5 min | **Cook Time:** 0 min | **Servings:** 2

- 2 peeled peaches
- 2 peeled kiwi
- 2 cups of coconut water
- the juice of one orange
- the juice of one lime
- 1 tablespoon of sesame seeds

Put all the ingredients in the blender with 8 ice cubes and blend on high speed for one minute.

Per serving: calories: 165 / fat: 3 / protein: 3 / carbs: 37 /

Smoothie With Green Cabbage And Apple

Prep Time: 5 min | **Cook Time:** 0 min | **Servings:** 2

- 1 cup of green cabbage
- 1 banana
- 1 apple
- 5 pitted dates
- 2 cups of unsweetened coconut milk

Put all the ingredients in the blender with 8 ice cubes and blend on high speed for one minute.

Per serving: calories: 216 / fat: 6 / protein: 2 / carbs: 46 /

| Smoothies & Juices

Smoothie With Oats And Apricots

Prep Time: 5 min
Cook Time: 0 min
Servings: 2

- 1 peeled pear
- 1 fennel
- 2 pitted apricots
- 1 tablespoon of raw honey
- 2 cups unsweetened oat milk

Put all the ingredients in the blender with 8 ice cubes and blend on high speed for one minute.

Per serving: calories: 183 / fat: 2 / protein: 3 / carbs: 38 /

Smoothie Tofu And Strawberries

Prep Time: 5 min
Cook Time: 0 min
Servings: 2

- 200 grams of tofu
- 1 cup of strawberries
- 1 kiwi
- 2 cups of oat milk

Put all the ingredients in the blender with 8 ice cubes and blend on high speed for one minute.

Per serving: calories: 167 / fat: 7 / protein: 8 / carbs: 24 /

Smoothie Mandarins And Grapefruit

Prep Time: 5 min **Cook Time:** 0 min **Servings:** 2

- 1 grapefruit without peel
- 2 pears
- 3 peeled tangerines
- 2 cups unsweetened coconut milk
- 1 teaspoon of maple syrup

Put all the ingredients in the blender with 8 ice cubes and blend on high speed for one minute.

Per serving: calories: 219 / fat: 5 / protein: 3 / carbs: 46 /

Smoothie With Lychees And Banana

Prep Time: 5 min **Cook Time:** 0 min **Servings:** 2

- 2 handfuls of peeled and pitted lychees
- 2 walnuts
- 1 banana
- a few leaves of fresh mint
- 1 teaspoon of maple syrup
- 2 cups unsweetened oat milk

Put all the ingredients in the blender with 8 ice cubes and blend on high speed for one minute.

Per serving: calories: 185 / fat: 4 / protein: 3 / carbs: 42 /

| Smoothies & Juices

Smoothie With Black Currants

Prep Time: 5 min
Cook Time: 0 min
Servings: 2

- 1 tablespoon of Brazilian nuts
- 5 tablespoons of oat flakes
- 1 teaspoon of cinnamon
- 1 cup of black currants
- 2 cups unsweetened almond milk

Put all the ingredients in the blender with 8 ice cubes and blend on high speed for one minute.

Per serving: calories: 138 / fat: 5 / protein: 3 / carbs: 24 /

Red Currant Juice

Prep Time: 5 min
Cook Time: 0 min
Servings: 2

- 200 grams of red currant
- 2 pears
- 1 lime
- 1 orange
- 1 cup of coconut water
- a few leaves of fresh mint

Put all the ingredients in the blender with 8 ice cubes and blend on high speed for one minute.

Per serving: calories: 208 / fat: 0 / protein: 7 / carbs: 55 /

Juice With Pomegranate And Raspberries

Prep Time 5 min | **Cook Time** 0 min | **Servings** 2

- the seeds of a pomegranate
- 3 dates
- 4 slices of pineapple
- 1 cup of coconut water
- 1 tablespoon of raspberries

Put all the ingredients in the blender with 8 ice cubes and blend on high speed for one minute.

Per serving: calories: 383 / fat: 3 / protein: 6 / carbs: 99 /

Juice With Winter Melon And Blueberries

Prep Time 5 min | **Cook Time** 0 min | **Servings** 2

- 1 cup of winter melon
- the juice of one lemon
- 1 cup of blueberries
- 2 tablespoons of coconut yogurt
- 1 cup of coconut water

Put all the ingredients in the blender with 8 ice cubes and blend on high speed for one minute.

Per serving: calories: 96 / fat: 1 / protein: 2 / carbs: 51 /

| Smoothies & Juices

Dessert

Chocolate And Cherries Cake

Prep Time 10 min **Cook Time** 35 min **Servings** 8

- 1 cup of pitted cherries
- 5 tablespoons of coconut milk
- 150 grams of wholemeal flour
- 150 grams of banana flour
- 90 grams of raw cocoa
- 5 tablespoons of maple syrup
- 1 teaspoon of gluten-free organic yeast
- 4 tablespoons of ghee
- 1 + 1/2 cup of oat milk

In a bowl, mix the wholemeal flour, banana flour, baking powder and cocoa. In another bowl, mix the maple syrup well with the ghee and oat milk. Mix the two compounds together. Heat the oven to 320° F. Line a pan with parchment paper and pour the mixture andadd the cherries. Cook for about 35 minutes.

Per serving: calories: 243 / fat: 6 / protein: 7 / carbs: 44 /

Yellow Cake

Prep Time 10 min **Cook Time** 25 min **Servings** 5

- 4 cups of oat milk
- 5 organic eggs
- 5 tablespoons of corn flour
- 5 tablespoons of maple syrup
- the zest of an organic orange

Put all the ingredients in the blender with 8 ice cubes and blend on high speed for one minute. Garnish with mint leaves and serve.

Per serving: calories: 166 / fat: 2 / protein: 3 / carbs: 36 /

Almond And Hazelnut Cake

Prep Time: 15 min | **Cook Time:** 20 min | **Servings:** 8

- 80 grams of wholemeal flour
- 80 grams of almond flour
- 1 teaspoon of salt
- 4 tablespoons of coconut butter
- 1 cup of rice milk
- 80 grams of chopped hazelnuts
- 80 grams of chopped almonds
- 1 cup of blueberries
- 1 tablespoon of maple syrup
- 2 cups of organic apple compote
- 1 teaspoon of vanilla extract

In a bowl, mix the wholemeal flour with the almond flour, baking soda and salt. Heat the milk and melt the coconut butter. Combine the two compounds and knead. Line a pan with parchment paper, spread the mixture inside the pan. Heat the oven to 350° F, place the pan in the oven and bake for 15 minutes. In a bowl, mix the chopped hazelnuts, almonds, blueberries, vanilla extract and compote. Pour over the cake and bake again for 3 minutes.

Per serving: calories: 324 / fat: 21 / protein: 8 / carbs: 27 /

Date And Apricot Cake

Prep Time: 10 min | **Cook Time:** 20 min | **Servings:** 9

- 100 grams of dried apricots
- 50 grams of dried and pitted dates
- 100 grams of dried papaya
- 3 cups unsweetened apple juice
- 1 tablespoon of raw honey
- 3 teaspoons of arrowroot
- 80 grams of wholemeal flour
- 80 grams of rice flour
- 1 teaspoon of salt
- 4 tablespoons of coconut butter
- 1 cup of rice milk

Pour 2 cups of apple juice into a bowl and soak the dried fruit for two hours. In a bowl, mix the wholemeal flour with the rice flour, baking soda and salt. Heat the milk and melt the coconut butter. Combine the two compounds and knead. Line a pan with parchment paper, spread the mixture inside the pan. Melt the arrowroot over moderate heat in the remaining cup of apple juice, when it is melted add the honey and mix. Arrange the dried and drained fruit in the pan, sprinkle with the arrowroot. Bake in the oven at 320° F for about 20 minutes.

Per serving: calories: 294 / fat: 10 / protein: 3 / carbs: 48 /

| Dessert

Beet Brownie

Prep Time: 10 min
Cook Time: 20 min
Servings: 8

- 500 grams of boiled beets
- 4 tablespoons of almond butter
- 200 grams of 70% dark chocolate
- 3 organic eggs
- 100 grams of buckwheat flour
- 1 tablespoon of raw cocoa
- 1 teaspoon of cardamom

Beat the eggs with the sugar. Put the well-drained beets in the mixer with the chocolate and butter and blend. Add the beet mixture to the eggs and flour and cocoa. Line a baking dish with parchment paper and pour the contents. Bake at 350° F for about 20 minutes. Cut into squares and serve.

Per serving: calories: 334 / fat: 18 / protein: 12 / carbos: 32 /

Wholemeal Rice Pudding With Plums

Prep Time: 10 min
Cook Time: 25 min
Servings: 3

- 1 cup of brown rice
- 4 cups of oat milk
- 1 tablespoon of maple syrup
- 1 pinch of salt
- 1 teaspoon of vanilla extract
- 2 organic eggs
- 5 dried and pitted plums

Put the rice in the oat milk with the vanilla, salt, syrup in a saucepan and cook over low heat. Stir often. Cook until the milk is completely absorbed and the rice is soft. Remove from heat. Beat eggs. Coarsely chop the plums. Incorporate the eggs into the rice, add the prunes and return to the heat over low heat for 1 minute.

Per serving: calories: 337 / fat: 14 / protein: 10 / carbos: 61 /

Pecan Walnut Pralines

Prep Time: 15 min
Cook Time: 0 min
Servings: 10

- 3 tablespoons of maple syrup
- 50 grams of grated coconut
- 1 teaspoon of vanilla extract
- 1 pinch of salt
- 3 tablespoons of almond butter
- 160 grams of pecans

Place all ingredients except almond butter and grated coconut in the blender and blend on high speed for one minute.
Mix with the coconut butter and shape into balls with your hands. Pass the balls in the coconut.

Per serving: calories: 148 / fat: 13 / protein: 2 / carbs: 5 /

Cake With Wild Berries

Prep Time: 10 min
Cook Time: 30 min
Servings: 6

- 90 grams of oat flakes
- 80 grams of rice flour
- 2 tablespoons of arrowroot
- 1 pinch of salt
- 3 tablespoons of ghee
- 4 tablespoons of raw honey
- 800 grams of mixed berries
- 1 organic lemon
- 1 teaspoon of vanilla extract

In a bowl, mix the salt, vanilla extract, flour, arrowroot and oat flakes. Combine the ghee and two tablespoons of honey and knead. Let the dough rest in a cling film in the refrigerator for about half an hour. Mix the berries with the lemon juice and two tablespoons of honey. Remove the dough from the fridge and spread it out in a pan lined with baking paper. Bake in a hot oven at 350° F for about 8 minutes. Remove from the oven and add the berries and cook for another 20 minutes.

Per serving: calories: 240 / fat: 4 / protein: 5 / carbs: 50 /

| Dessert

Chocolate Cream With Kiwi And Hazelnuts

Prep Time: 10 min | **Cook Time:** 15 min | **Servings:** 5

- 1 cup of coconut milk
- 1 teaspoon of vanilla extract
- 2 tablespoons of coconut butter
- 2 organic egg yolks
- 2 spoons of agave syrup
- 1 pinch of salt
- 100 grams of 70% dark chocolate
- 1/2 cup of soy yogurt
- 2 kiwis
- 10 hazelnuts

In a saucepan, heat the coconut milk with the coconut butter and vanilla extract. When it is lukewarm, add the chocolate and mix until it is completely melted. Beat the egg yolks with the agave syrup and salt. In a bowl, transfer the chocolate mixed with milk and the eggs, mix well. Put the cream in the glasses and distribute the diced kiwi and chopped hazelnuts.

Per serving: calories: 245 / fat: 17 / protein: 4 / carbs: 23 /

Cookies With Peanut Butter And Sesame Seeds

Prep Time: 10 min | **Cook Time:** 8 min | **Servings:** 8

- 150 grams of almond flour
- 150 grams of wholemeal flour
- 1 teaspoon of baking soda
- 1 teaspoon of raw cocoa
- 1 pinch of salt
- 5 tablespoons of peanut butter
- 3 tablespoons of sesame seeds
- 2 tablespoons of maple syrup
- 3 tablespoons of almond butter

Mix the almond flour, wholemeal flour, baking soda, vanilla extract, salt and cocoa. Add the peanut butter, sesame seeds, maple syrup and almond butter and knead. Shape into balls with your hands and crush them. Line a baking sheet with parchment paper, spread the cookies on the baking sheet and bake at 330° F for about 8 minutes.

Per serving: calories: 226 / fat: 14 / protein: 8 / carbs: 17 /

Baked Apples With Crumble

Prep Time: 10 min
Cook Time: 20 min
Servings: 16

- 8 apples
- 1 teaspoon of grated ginger root
- 1 teaspoon of cinnamon
- 200 grams of pecans
- 180 grams of oat flakes
- 3 teaspoons of sesame
- 3 teaspoons of grated dried coconut
- 1 pinch of salt
- 5 tablespoons of ghee
- 5 tablespoons of maple syrup
- 2 organic lemons

Peel and cut the apples into wedges. Line a pan with parchment paper and distribute the apple wedges inside. Squeeze the lemon juice, mix it with the cinnamon and ginger root and sprinkle over the apples. Bake at 350° F for 10 minutes. Meanwhile, in a bowl, mix the chopped pecans, coarsely chopped oat flakes in the blender, salt, maple syrup, ghee, sesame and coconut. Make large crumbs with your hands, remove the apples from the oven and sprinkle the crumbs. Bake again for about 10 minutes.

Per serving: calories: 237 / fat: 13 / protein: 4 / carbs: 30 /

Ice Cream Cake With Raspberries

Prep Time: 15 min
Cook Time: 0 min
Servings: 8

- 2 cups of raspberries
- 250 grams of peanut cookies (see recipe)
- 2 tablespoons of coconut butter
- 3 cups of coconut yogurt
- 1 tablespoon of maple syrup
- 1 tablespoon of 70% dark chocolate
- the juice of an organic lemon

Blend the raspberries together with the maple syrup and lemon juice. Finely crumble the biscuits and mix them with the coconut butter.
Put the crumbled biscuits in a baking dish, spread the yogurt mixed with the lampini sauce on top. Cover with chocolate and place in the freezer for a couple of hours.

Per serving: calories: 287 / fat: 22 / protein: 7 / carbs: 15 /

| Dessert

Apricot Cake

Prep Time: 15 min
Cook Time: 25 min
Servings: 8

- 250 grams of wholemeal flour
- 250 grams of almond flour
- 3/4 cup of rice milk
- 1 teaspoon of salt
- 1 tablespoon of chopped pecans
- 1 tablespoon of chopped hazelnuts
- 4 dried apricots cut into small pieces
- 4 tablespoons of almond butter

Mix the two flours with the almond butter, the water, the milk and the salt, mix well and let the dough rest closed in a cling film for about half an hour. After this time, roll out the dough and put the pecans, hazelnuts and apricots in the center, knead again. Leave to rest for 10 minutes. Roll out the dough into a lightly greased ovenproof dish and bake in a hot oven at 350° F for about 25 minutes.

Per serving: calories: 325 / fat: 20 / protein: 10 / carbs: 25 /

Pumpkin And Dates Cake

Prep Time: 15 min
Cook Time: 20 min
Servings: 8

- 100 grams of wholemeal flour
- 50 grams of almond flour
- 4 cups boiled cubed squash
- 4 apples, peeled and cut into wedges
- 4 pitted dates
- 1 teaspoon of coconut butter

Mix the flours. Put the pumpkin and dates in the blender and blend. Mix the flours with the date and pumpkin cream. Grease a pan, pour in the mixture and decorate with the sliced apples standing in the dough. Bake at 400° F for about 20 minutes.

Per serving: calories: 170 / fat: 4 / protein: 4 / carbs: 32 /

Mint Chocolates

Prep Time: 15 min
Cook Time: 0 min
Servings: 20

- 160 grams of dried and grated coconut
- 80 grams of almond flour
- 1 teaspoon of maple syrup
- 1 teaspoon of raw honey
- 140 grams of coconut oil
- 140 grams of ghee
- 2 tablespoons of 70% dark cocoa powder
- 2 tablespoons of powdered mint extract

Mix and blend all the ingredients in the blender. Pour the cream into chocolate molds and refrigerate for three hours.

Per serving: calories: 186 / fat: 16 / protein: 2 / carbs: 4 /

Sorbet With Honey And Goji Berries

Prep Time: 15 minutes + 160 minutes waiting time
Cook Time: 0 min
Servings: 2

- 5 tablespoons of raw honey
- 3 tablespoons of goji berries
- 1 cup of water

Soak the goji berries for about 30 minutes, drain well. Bring the cup of water to a boil and dissolve the honey. Allow to cool and add the goji berries. Place in a container and place in the freezer for about 30 minutes. Remove from the freezer, mix well and put it back in the freezer for 30 minutes. Repeat 5 times.

Per serving: calories: 175 / fat: 0 / protein: 0 / carbs: 47 /

| Dessert

Peach Muffin

Prep Time: 10 min
Cook Time: 25 min
Servings: 4

- 2 peeled and diced peaches
- 75 grams of almond flour
- 75 grams of wholemeal flour
- 3 tablespoons of agave syrup
- 2 cups of oats milk
- 3 tablespoons of coconut butter
- 1 teaspoon of organic yeast
- 2 organic eggs

Mix the flours with the yeast. Beat the eggs and stir in the coconut butter and agave syrup. In a bowl, combine the milk with the flour, mix and add the eggs. Also add the peaches. Pour the mixture into the muffin molds, filling them three quarters full. bake at 350° F for about 25 minutes.

Per serving: calories: 381 / fat: 19 / protein: 12 / carbs: 45 /

Ice Lollies With Cherry And Kiwi

Prep Time: 10 min
Cook Time: 0 min
Servings: 4

- 1 kiwi
- 5 pitted cherries
- 2 cups of coconut milk
- 1 tablespoon of raw honey

Peel the kiwifruit and put all the ingredients in the blender. Blend on high speed for about one minute. Transfer the mixture to the popsicle molds and place in the freezer.

Per serving: calories: 61 / fat: 2 / protein: 1 / carbs: 1 /

Pears Cake

Prep Time: 10 min
Cook Time: 30 min
Servings: 6

- 125 grams of buckwheat flour
- 125 grams of almond flour
- 800 grams of peeled and diced pears
- 1 cup of coconut yogurt
- 50 grams of rice flour
- 50 grams of banana flour
- 3 tablespoons of water
- 5 tablespoons of maple syrup
- 1 teaspoon ground cinnamon
- 4 tablespoons of coconut oil
- 1 teaspoon of baking soda

Mix all the flours with the cinnamon and baking soda. Add the water and maple syrup, add the coconut oil, the yogurt, and mix well. Finally, incorporate the pears. Line a pan with parchment paper and pour the dough, bake in a hot oven at 350° F for about 30 minutes.

Per serving: calories: 395 / fat: 15 / protein: 10 / carbs: 59 /

Chestnut And Chocolate Cookies

Prep Time: 10 min
Cook Time: 15 min
Servings: 14

- 120 grams of chestnut flour
- 240 grams of rice flour
- 1 teaspoon of organic yeast
- 1 pinch of salt
- 4 tablespoons of arrowroot
- 4 tablespoons of coconut oil
- 100 grams of 70% dark chocolate chips
- 1 peeled pear

Mix the flours with the baking powder, salt and arrowroot. Chop the chocolate and blend the pear. Combine all the ingredients and knead. Shape into balls with your hands and crush them. Place them on a baking sheet with parchment paper and bake at 350° F for about 15 minutes.

Per serving: calories: 107 / fat: 3 / protein: 1 / carbs: 19 /

| Dessert

61 Days Meal Plan

NOTE: This meal plan is only meant to be a generic example. Each person is different and needs a different amount of daily calories based on age, height, and work or study.

DAY	BREAKFAST	SNACK	LUNCH	DINNER	TOT CALORIES
1	Morning hazelnut piadine	Sesame and paprika crackers	almon with rocket pesto+Eggplant and pomegranate salad+Banana muffin	opinambur and potato soup+caramelized rape	1,719
2	Dried fruit breakfast bar	Spirulina smoothie	Spinach and broccoli soup+ Millet meatballs+Pumpkin and dates cake	Squid rings with saffron+autumn salad	1,409
3	Soy cream with asparagus+Red currant juice	Apple and cinnamon chips	Radish and hazelnut salad+Wholemeal pasta with avocado and apple+Strawberries lemon and mint	Pastinache with broccoli cream+Seaweed fritters nori and carrots	1,515
4	Millet cake with plums+Goji berry salad+Smoothie with green cabbage and apple	Cookies with peanut butter and sesame seeds	Salad of cucumber and soy yogurt+Buckwheat gnocchi wit salmon and shrimps	Soup of black beans and zucchini	1,570
5	Pumpkin swee+ Beet and mango smoothie	Turmeric focaccia with nuts	Spicy salad+Barley, tomato, capers and anchovies+Green tea and dark chocolate mousse	Cod in grapefruit cups+Rösti potatoes with rosemary	1,631
6	Basket of lentils and carrots+Almond and hazelnut cake	Peanut Butter toast with vegetables	Couscous with mixed vegetables+Avocado stuffed with spicy chickpeas and tofu	Buckwheat with pistachios and raisins	1,690
7	Pudding of apricots and hazelnut+Smoothie mandarins and grapefruits	Algae chips	Salmon salad with mushrooms and broccoli+Artichoke flan+potato croquettes with pumpkin seeds	Quinoa with tuna and pesto	1,451
8	Oat flakes with pears and blueberries+Date and apricots cake	Baked apples with crumble	Basmati rice with peppers+Green beans with coconut and almonds	Cauliflower and tempeh soup	1,455
9	Muffin with spinach and cayenne pepper+Almond and orange smoothie	Chocolate and cherries cake	Cod with creamy onions+Quenelle of cannellini beans with hummus and parsley cream	Tempeh with olives and capers	1,620

Anti inflammatory Diet Cookbook for Beginners 2022

DAY	BREAKFAST	SNACK	LUNCH	DINNER	TOT CALORIES
10	Brown rice cream+Juice with pomegranate and raspberries	Apricots cake	Hamburger of black rice and chickpeas+Celery with curry sauce+ Crunchy balls of garlic potatoes	Green beans and pine nuts salad	1,388
11	Pudding with black currant and mint+exotic salad	Banana and hazelnut cookies+Mango and dragon fruit smoothie	Piadine of chickpeas with spinach and mayonnaise+ chutney of red onions and apple+Ice cream with raspberries	Salt cake with asparagus and mushroom cream+Watermelon and lemongrass smoothie	1,417
12	Frittata with zucchini+Green smoothie	Chocolate cream with kiwi and hazelnut	Brown rice with tuna, peppers and rocket+Fennel and celery salad+Pecan walnut pralines	Saffron artichokes soup	1,305
13	Quinoa bread with pecan walnut butter+Spinach with leek and hazelnuts+Juice with winter melon and blueberries	Oat bars with cocoa and honey	Mackerel with sesame and soy sprouts+Cream of lentils and sweet potatoes	Wholemeal rise with pumpkin, ghee and nuts	1,583
14	Banana pancakes with apricots+Papaya and pineapple smoothie	Quinoa and lemon cookies	Millet with asparagus, almond and sardines+tomatoes stuffed with tuna and chickpeas	Pearl barley and red beans soup	1,301
15	Cake with wild berries+Smoothie with oats and apricots	Stick with sesame and turmeric	Seitan stew with olives+Artichokes and pears salad+Sweet potatoes in sweet sour sauce	Pomegranate and pistachio soup+Artichokes and beet frittata	1,465
16	Salad of pastinaca and red beans+Tofu and strawberries smoothie	Pear and cinnamon pudding	Turmeric sandwiches+Greek salad+mint chocolates	Wholemeal pasta with tofu, pine nuts and leek+Nugget of zucchini	1,304
17	Fresh summer salad+Morning smoothie	Peach muffin	Farro with grilled vegetables+Cabbage with anchovies	Soup of mushrooms and tempeh	1,416
18	Cucumber and pomegranate salad+Beet and apple smoothie	Skewers of tofu and zucchini	Buckwheat with broccoli, zucchini and aubergines+Sorbet with honey and Goji berries	Salad of celeriac+Buckwheat soup and onions	1,435
19	Orange stuffed with banana and blueberries+Peaches and kiwi smoothie+Brown rice cream	Cake with carrots and chocolate	Sole fillets with fennel in paperboard+Curry pastiche cream with leek and black beans	Wholemeal spaghetti with pears, cashews and asparagus +zucchini fritters with garlic sauce	1,596

DAY	BREAKFAST	SNACK	LUNCH	DINNER	TOT CALORIES
20	Mixed salad with quinoa bread+Smoothie with black currant	Beet brownie	Wholemeal pasta and Shiitake mushrooms+white onion filled with rice	Quinoa with figs and peppers	1,451
21	Salad of fennel, pecan and blueberries+Almond and carrots smoothie	Yellow cake	Hake with caper sauce and dried tomatoes+Aromatic salad+Baked apple with crumble	Orange soup+Kamut with green beans and saffron mushrooms	1,374
22	Pears cake+Strawberries Hazelnut smoothie	Sesame and paprika crackers	Rolls of quinoa, lettuce and raspberry+Bean soup and lemon	Barley, olives and tofu	1,381
23	Piadine with tofu and pesto+Smoothie mandarins and grapefruit	Turmeric focaccia with nuts	Clams with chickpeas+Crunchy balls of garlic potatoes	Spicy quinoa cauliflower and almonds	1,497
24	Morning hazelnut piadine+Red currant juice	Peanut Butter toast with vegetables	Wholemeal pasta with walnut pesto, pecan, basil and dried tomatoes+Caramelized rape with hazelnut	Chestnut and bean soup	1,409
25	Salt cake with asparagus and mushroom cream+Smoothie Lychees and banana	Millet cake with plums	Wholemeal spaghetti with cod and parsley and garlic sauce+ artichokes flan	Bulgur with edamame beans and sprouts	1,209
26	Oat flakes with pears and blueberries+Acai smoothie+Pistachio and pecan walnuts granola for breakfast	Sauce for croutons with salmon+Stick with sesame and turmeric	Pasta with chestnut rogout+Avocado stuffed with spicy chickpeas and tofu	Spicy pumpkin soup	1,603
27	Basket of lentils and carrots+Beet and mango smoothie	Exotic salad	Millet with tuna and broccoli+Rocked and asparagus salad	Turnip and spelled soup+Green beans with coconut and almonds	1,361
28	Soy cream with asparagus+Strawberries lemon and mint	Smoothie with green cabbage and apple	Wholemeal pasta with zucchini flowers, tomatoes, anchovies and pine nut+Tempeh with ginger sauce	Pumpkin with miso and nut+Zucchini filled with hummus and spinach	1,350
29	Crepes with chickpeas and spinach+Spirulina smoothie and fresh mint	Chocolate cream with kiwi and hazelnut	Spelled pasta with grapes and lemon+Seaweed fritters nori and carrots	Broccoli and pears soup	1,281
30	Dried fruits breakfast bars+Juice with pomegranate and raspberries	Almond and hazelnut cake	Greek feta with tomatoes and almond pesto+Spinach with leek and hazelnut	Rolls of aubergines with cod with mediterranean aromas	1,440

DAY	BREAKFAST	SNACK	LUNCH	DINNER	TOT CALORIES
31	Cookies with peanut butter and sesame seeds+Mango and dragon fruit smoothie	Banana and hazelnut cookies	Cod and pumpkin fishballs with white sauce+Tuna croutons	Sweet potato carpaccio with cremini mushrooms cream+Potato croquettes with pumpkin seeds	1,306
32	Pudding of apricots and hazelnuts+Almond and orange smoothie	Apple and cinnamon chips+Celery with curry sauce	Rice paper rolls with broccoli and tofu+Tomatoes stuffed with tuna and chickpeas	Wholemeal pasta with sardines and leeks	1,209
33	Pumpkin cake+Mandarins and grapefruit smoothie	Peanut butter toast with vegetables	Quinoa with totani dried tomatoes and chickpeas+Seaweed fritters nori and carrots	Soup of black beans and zucchini+Sesame and paprika crackers	1,408
34	Morning hazelnut piadine+Strawberries lemon and mint	Juice with pomegranate and raspberries	Pasta with anchovies, broccoli and pecan nuts+Salmon salad with mushrooms and broccoli	Squid rings with saffron	1,665
35	BREAKFAST: Salmon with rocket pesto+Banana muffin	Peaches and kiwi smoothie	Farro with zucchini, tuna and leek+Salad with red cabbage	Spinach and cornflour soup+Nugget of zucchini	1,349
36	Oat bars with cocoa and honey+Smoothie with green cabbage and apple	Pudding with black currant and milk	Wholemeal pasta with avocado and apple+green beans with coconut and almonds	Topinambur and potato soup+Crunchy balls of garlic potatoes	1,688
37	Salad of cucumber and so yogurt+Pear and cinnamon pudding	Watermelon and lemongrass smoothie+Algae chips	Cod with creamy onions+Turmeric focaccia with nuts	Hamburger of black rice and chickpeas	1,372
38	Frittata with zucchini+Brown rice cream	Muffin with spinach and cayenne pepper	Lentils and turmeric soup+Quenelle of cannellini beans with hummus and parsley cream	Tempeh with olives ad capers+Radish and hazelnut salad+Ice cream with raspberries	1,515
39	Apricot cake	Strawberries and hazelnut smoothie+Pistachio and pecan walnuts granola	Spicy salad+Buckwheit gnocchi with salmon and shrimps	Venus rice with mackerel and tomatoes	1,434
40	Banana pancakes with apricots+Almond and coconut smoothie	Apple and cinnamon chips+Juice with pomegranate and raspberries	Piadine of chickpeas with spinach and mayonnaise +Eggplant and pomegranate salad	Spinach and kale soup+Turmeric focaccia with nuts	1,675
41	Dried fruit breakfast bars+Beet and mango smoothie	Chocolate and carrots cake	Meatballs with millet and broccoli+Cabbage with anchovies	Potato croquettes with pumpkin seeds+Quinoa with tuna and pesto	1,634

DAY	BREAKFAST	SNACK	LUNCH	DINNER	TOT CALORIES
42	Oat flakes with pears and blueberries+Smoothie with black currant	Millet cake with plums	Rice with aubergines and octopus+Curry pastiche cream with leek and black beans	Buckwheat with pistachios and raisins+Caramelized rape with hazelnut	1,510
43	Morning hazelnut piadine	Smoothie papaya and pineapple	Baked wholemeal pasta gratin+Autumn salad	Basmati rice with peppers+Date and apricots cake	1,467
44	Dried fruits breakfast bars+Smoothie tofu and strawberries	Rösti potatoes with rosemary	Zucchini fritters with garlic sauce+Chestnut panini with fennel	Wholemeal rice with cod and pine nuts	1,353
45	Baskets of lentils and carrots	Smoothie with oats and apricots+Sesame and paprika crackers	Salmon salad with mushrooms and broccoli+Tuna croutons	Barley tomato, capers and anchovies+Baked apples with crumble	1,371
46	Soy cream with asparagus+Turmeric focaccia with nuts	Banana muffin+Green smoothie	Sole fillets with fennel in paperboard+Green beans and pine nuts salad+Quinoa bread	Asparagus and Tamari soup+Salt cake with asparagus and mushrooms cream	1,586
47	Crepes of chickpeas and spinach+ Goji berries salad	Red currant juice+Banana and hazelnut cookies	Bulgur with edamame beans and sprouts+Cream of lentils and sweet potatoes	Quenelle of cannellini beans with hummus and parsley cream+Sick with sesame and turmeric	1,654
48	Muffin with spinach and cayenne pepper+Salad of fennel, pecan and blueberries	Quinoa and lemon cookies+Juice with winter melon and blueberries	Cous cous with mixed vegetables+Sweet potatoes in sweet and sour sauce	Millet with tuna and broccoli+Chocolate and cherries cake	1,576
49	Banana pancakes with apricots+Green tea and dark chocolate mousse	Beet and apple smoothie	Meatballs with millet and broccoli+Avocado stuffed with spicy chickpeas and tofu	White onion filled with rice+ Chestnut panini with fennel	1,243
50	Quinoa bread with pecan walnut butter+Sauce for croutons with salmon	Skewers of tofu and zucchini	Cod with creamy onions+Quinoa bread	Spelled pasta with grapes and lemon+Artichokes flan	1,669
51	Pudding of apricots and hazelnuts+Sesame and paprika crackers	Almond and hazelnuts cake+Spirulina smoothie and fresh mint	Mackerel with sesame and soy sprouts+Tuna croutons	Cauliflowers and tempeh soup+Seaweed fritters nori and carrots	1,649
52	Frittata with zucchini+Stick with sesame and turmeric	Beet brownie+Smoothie with lychees and banana	Cod and pumpkin fishballs with white sauce+Quinoa bread	Farro with grilled vegetables+Crunchy balls of garlic potatoes	1,660

DAY	BREAKFAST	SNACK	LUNCH	DINNER	TOT CALORIES
53	Pudding with black currant and mint+Juice of pomegranate and raspberries	Peanut Butter toast with vegetables	Cod in grapefruit cups+Barley, olives and tofu	Wholemeal pasta with tofu, pine nuts and leek+Yellow cake	1,675
54	Oat flakes with pears and blueberries+Chocolate cream with kiwi and hazelnut	Beet and mango smoothie	Salmon with rocket pesto+Chestnut panini with fennel	Clams with chickpeas+Pastinache with broccoli cream	1,671
55	Brown rice cream+Green tea and dark chocolate mousse	Smoothie with green cabbage and apple	Wholemeal pasta with zucchini flowers tomatoes, anchovies and pine nuts+Eggplant and pomegranate salad	Wholemeal rice with pumpkin, ghee and nuts+Spinach with leek and hazelnuts	1,414
56	Morning hazelnut piadine	Chocolate and cherries cake+Smoothie oats and apricots	Hake with caper sauce and dried tomatoes+Turmeric focaccia with nuts	Seitan stew with olives+Algae chips	1,352
57	Millet cake with plums+Peaches and kiwi smoothie	Cake with carrots and chocolate	Piadine of chickpeas with spinach+Artichokes and pears salad	Buckwheat soup and onions+Sorbet with honey and Goji berries	1,472
58	Dried fruit breakfast bars	Wholemeal rice pudding with plums	Spicy quinoa cauliflower and almonds+Rocket and asparagus salad	Spinach and broccoli soup+Artichokes and beet frittata	1,325
59	Soy cream with asparagus+Quinoa bread	Cake with wild berry+Smoothie with mandarins and grapefruits	Venus rice with mackerel and tomatoes+Fennel and celery salad	Turnip and spelled soup+Tempeh with ginger sauce	1,547
60	Muffin with spinach and caienna peppers+Red currant juice	Sesame and paprika crackers+Chutney of red onions and apple	Salmon salad with mushrooms and broccoli+Chestnut panini with fennel	Wholemeal rice with cod and pine nuts+Salad of cucumber and soy yogurt	1,423
61	Cookies with peanut butter and sesame seeds+Acai smoothie	Sesame and paprika crackers+Sauce for croutons with salmon	Mixed salad with quinoa bread+Broccoli and brown pear soup+Ice cream with raspberries	Wholemeal pasta with avocado and apple+Greek feta with tomatoes and almond pesto	1,870

| 61 Days Meal Plan

FAQ

What is the anti-inflammatory diet?

The anti-inflammatory diet is a way of eating that focuses on foods that reduce inflammation in the body. Inflammation is a natural process that helps the body heal and protect itself from harm. However, when it becomes chronic, it can lead to a number of health problems. The anti-inflammatory diet can help to reduce chronic inflammation and promote overall health.

What are the benefits of the anti-inflammatory diet?

The anti-inflammatory diet has been shown to provide a number of health benefits, including reducing the risk of chronic diseases such as heart disease, stroke, cancer, and Alzheimer's disease. Additionally, the diet can help to improve joint health, reduce pain and stiffness, and promote healthy skin.

What foods should I eat on the anti-inflammatory diet?

There are a variety of foods that can help reduce inflammation in the body. These include fruits, vegetables, whole grains, fish and olive oil. And, of course, all the recipes written in this book. Also, it's important to avoid processed foods, sugar, and refined carbohydrates.

How important are calories in the anti-inflammatory diet?

The calories we eat are not all the same, for example 100 calories of seeds do not have the same effect on our body as 100 calories given by industrial snacks. The anti-inflammatory diet is a path to a healthy lifestyle, which gives your body the tools to stay healthy and therefore achieve a healthy weight.

Canned food, yes or no?

My advice is not to seek perfection at any cost. Wanting to be perfect, never fail, will soon lead to abandoning all good intentions. Every day try to do the best you can. If you don't have time to cook, take advantage of canned food, nothing serious will happen!

Why are there no meat and poultry recipes in this book?

Many studies have shown that the consumption of meat increases the inflammatory state of our body, for this reason there are no recipes that provide for the consumption of meat. However, as we said earlier, perfection is not necessary. If sometimes you want to have a barbecue with friends, nothing serious will happen.

Is the anti-inflammatory diet more expensive?

It might seem like a healthier lifestyle is more expensive, but it's really all a matter of organization. Local markets are a good place to shop and supermarkets always have offers. Buying larger quantities and freezing food can also be a good strategy. Plus, your health is priceless.

Conversion Table

CUPS	METRICS
1/4 cup	60 ml
1/3 cup	70 ml
1/2 cup	125 ml
2/3 cup	150 ml
3/4 cup	175 ml
1 cup	250 ml

OVEN TEMPERATURE

CELSIUS	FAHRENHEIT	GAS	DESCRIPTION
110 °C	230 °F	1/4	Cool
120 °C	250 °F	1/2	Cool
140 °C	275 °F	1	Very low
150 °C	300 °F	2	Very low
160 °C	325 °F	3	Low
170 °C	338 °F	3	Moderate
180 °C	350 °F	4	Moderate
190 °C	375 °F	5	Moderately Hot
200 °C	400 °F	6	Hot

WEIGHT

METRIC	IMPERIAL	METRIC	IMPERIAL
5 gr	1/8 oz	100 gr	3 1/2 oz
10 gr	1/4 oz	150 gr	5 1/2 oz
15 gr	1/2 oz	200 gr	7 oz
20 gr	3/4 oz	250 gr	9 oz
25 gr	1 oz	300 gr	10 1/2 oz
35 gr	1 1/4 oz	350 gr	12 oz
40 gr	1 1/2 oz	400 gr	14 oz
50 gr	1 3/4 oz	425 gr	15 oz

MEASURE EQUIVALENTS

CUP	TBSP	TSP	FLUID OZ	MILLIMETER
1	16	48	8	237
3/4	12	36	6	177
2/3	10+2 tsp	32	5+1/3	158
1/2	8	24	4	118
1/3	5+1 tsp	16	2+2/3	79
1/4	4	12	2	59

REFERENCES

1- https://www.bmj.com/content/365/bmj.l2110

2- https://retinafoundation.org/wp-content/uploads/2016/02/Antioxidants-in-Foods.pdf

3- https://pubmed.ncbi.nlm.nih.gov/26400429/

4- https://www.ncbi.nlm.nih.gov/pmc/articles/PMC8389628/

AUTHOR: Lora M. Stoops

Manufactured by Amazon.ca
Bolton, ON